The World's Best Clean Jokes:

The Ultimate Encyclopedia of Humor.

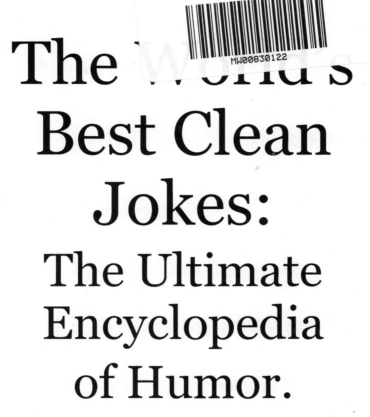

Christopher James

Branson, Missouri, USA

The World's Best Clean Jokes: The Ultimate Encyclopedia of Humor.

Printed in the United States of America

ISBN: 978-0-9855789-4-7

Learn more information at: funnyhypermagic.com

Dedicated to my wife, Rachael, our twins, Alexander and Cassandra, and the one girl that can always make me laugh and smile, Olivia Vanessa

Contents

Welcome to my complete encyclopedia of comedy. I've released this volume as a collection of my major books and publications to date. I'm particularly proud of my book of one-liners. Over the years, I have had man interested and improvised moments on stage while performing over 500 shows a year. Being the obsessed person I am, I kept careful records of each and every new joke. This includes regulars in my live show and many that were off the cuff. Gathering them together, I realized I had enough to make my own new book. I decided combining them with my other joke books would make the ultimate collection of humor for any situation and age. Thus, this book was born.

There is never a shortage of material as a professional comedian. I find humor in every day life and situations, sometimes to the dismay of those around me. It's a gift and a curse. Over the years, I have found a career in comedy to not only be therapeutic, but also very rewarding. People are never shy about sharing a joke or a funny anecdote after a show. One thing I have learned, everyone loves to laugh.

Anyone that has ever seen my show knows that I like to have something for everyone. I include jokes for every age, lifestyle, and intellectual level. I like to include simple puns and anecdotes and few jokes that will make the audience think.

This book is a compilation of many things. First, it's jokes, stories and anecdotes I've collected over the years from audience members and friends. Second, it's my own style of humor and jokes from my show and personal life. Third, there are some jokes that I have purchased from professionals over the years. And last, it's some of the stories and jokes that have been passed down from generation to generation. Some oldies but goodies that still bring a smile, no matter how corny.

I've organized this book in the style of my own show. A mixture that will leave you thinking one minute, groaning the next, and laughing a paragraph later. Not every joke is for everyone. However, I feel there is something for everyone.

Enjoy.

Christopher's Ultimate Collection of One Liners, Observations, and Jokes

Christopher James

Branson, Missouri, USA

If life gives you melons, you must be dyslexic

Shout out to this ATM fee for making me buy my own money.

I hate waiting in lines. I wish this lady would hurry up and pick a suspect already.

Do you brush your teeth without making a mess like in the commercials? Because I usually look like I have minty fresh rabies....

Don't get your panties in a bunch. The nicer ones are sold individually.

My uncle was a parsley farmer. Unfortunately, his wages were always garnished.

If a farmer breaks up with his tractor, does he get a John Deere letter instead of a Dear John letter?

We figured out I had dyslexia when I went to a toga party dressed as a goat.

I would like to dedicate this trick to all the ladies in the audience, and I think you know who you are.

Let's be honest, Chuck E Cheese is nothing more than a casino for kids.

I used to own a Mexican restaurant called The A-Taco-Lypse. It went great until we tried to advertise our diet margaritas called Dia-ritas.

Clowns aren't scary. One has been staring at me thru the window all night. I can't stop giggling at the balloon chainsaw he's making.

Facebook has allowed me to bring my "He's a distraction to the rest of the class" from grade school to a global scale.

I have decided to write all his statuses in capitals from now on. This one was written in London.

Fajitas are the IKEA of Mexican foods.

If you think writing in the proper tense is difficult now, just wait until time travel was possible.

A crazy woman tried to chase down my car as I left the mall. Maybe it was the previous owner. She looked a lot like the baby in the backseat

No. I do. I think your baby is adorable. I'm just concerned about what might happen if you get it wet or let it eat after midnight.

I have serious ethical problems participating in human cloning experiments. I just couldn't live with myself.

Dude. Go shave your mustache. Just because it looks good on your mother doesn't mean you can wear it well.

I'm disappointed in you, Santa. Is that how you talk to every grown man who cries on your lap? ...I'm not happy with mall security either.

It's high time we change the name of the Indian Ocean to Native American Ocean

I don't buy fat-free milk because I don't want to encourage cows with body image issues.

I hopped out of bed this morning like Fred Astaire. Or anyone else, really, who has been dead for 20 years.

My family reunion is like a bus ride. I want it to end as quickly as possible, preferably with nobody talking to me.

I've been waiting in line at the DMV so long, someone just stapled a lost cat flyer to my chest.

If tomatoes are technically a fruit, is ketchup technically a smoothie?

So sad America ranks 25th in the world in math. But at least we're still in the top 10.

Business idea: a home surgery kit called Suture Self.

Short in the front, long in the back... pickup trucks are the mullets of automobiles.

Of all the possible utensils that could have been invented to eat rice with... How did 2 sticks win out!?

Another World's Oldest Man has died. This is beginning to look suspicious. His mother was devastated.

Every warning label has an awesome backstory.

The say you should test your fire alarm once a month. I try but it's costing me a fortune in houses.

If you quit school, just remember two things.

1. You tried your best, and

2. I don't like pickles on my Big Mac.

No, I don't want to come to your cat's birthday party...you freak.

My dog's getting married that weekend.

Every Olympic event should include one average person competing, for reference.

I hate when people incinerate that I don't know how to use big words.

As I watched the dog chasing his tail, I thought, "Dogs are easily amused." Then I realized I was watching the dog chase his tail.

Next time you order coffee at Starbucks tell them your name is Bueller and then leave the store.

He said, "Your obsession with cats is out of control. I can't handle it anymore."

She cried, "You're kicking meeeowt?"

Maybe we should be focusing less on Goldilocks and more on why Mama and Papa bear don't sleep in the same bed anymore.

My wife and I laugh at how competitive we are at things, but I laugh more.

We hate what we do not understand. I'm not really sure what that phrase means, but it's stupid!

Relax. If you didn't want me knocking it over, why the hell did you write "tip jar" on it? Just for that, I'm taking my 15 cents back.

You wouldn't think any of my tweets were funny if you knew how many pedestrians I injured while writing them.

I hope you all like me half as much as I do

Today is the Deam to carpe

I'm not trying to showoff, I'm just trying to show you things I can do and no one else can.

Wow you aren't the sharpest knife in the place you keep knives

Knock Knock jokes are nothing more than gateway jokes to the heavier stuff.

I renamed my computer "that thang". I'm constantly reminded to back "that thang" up.

I was raised my mimes. I've seen unspeakable things

I get paid to do things that get most people committed.

Wow, that was impressive. What other activities are you not good at?

Why do we only get two choices when electing a president but 50 for Ms. America?

Some people like to give you a clue as to what is happening. I am clueless.

If my doctor brother is so great, why has he killed five people and I've only killed two as a comedian?

You won't see a CSI show set in the deep south. All the DNA is the same, and there are no dental records.

All the dominoes are falling like a house of cards. Checkmate.

If that's his trophy wife, he must have just got an honorable mention.

We don't call them rednecks here, we call them country music star

-You know what it means if Charlie Sheen see his shadow? Two more months of rehab.

I want people to laugh when I walk in and applaud when I leave.

Come on people, this is not rocket surgery. Work with me here.

I may not be the sharpest knife in the crayon box...

It's Chinese New Year already? I'll still be writing Year of the Snake on my checks for months.

Do what I do, fill up rental cars with a garden hose.

Gas prices are so high, it's cheaper to just call a tow truck to pull me around.

I'm starting a new dating service for my older fans called carbon dating.

Thank you for applauding what my parents are ashamed of. My she is one opinion away from being replaced.

I have a cat named chairman meow. He's very territorial.

Come on people, we are wasting valueless time.

Someone just picked an entire bouquet of oopsie daisies.

I've done more shows than I can count. Because I do a ton of shows, not because I can't count very high.

Not not laughing is not going to make that any better

We will now be dimming lights to enhance the appearance of our cast.

We lost my grandmother in 2001, and then she died on 2006

My grandma always wanted to be buried with her favorite things. Her cat was not happy.

I have a framed Harvard diploma with my name on it, which proves I am good at Photoshop.

I became a father recently. Yes, I decided to join the priesthood

I went to a four year olds birthday party yesterday and it was so awkward. Probably because I wasn't invited.

Later on when these jokes are explained to you, you will laugh so hard.

I am so going to make you a mix tape. Do you like Phil Collins?

Never leave alphabet soup on the stove. It could spell trouble.

Was your shirt a gift? No? You mean you paid for that??

A movie ticket should cost $100 for a baby

When someone invites you to their wedding, don't tell them "you can't go but you'll go to the next one"

I don't care who you are. If a kid wants to show you something they are proud of, you act impressed.

Kids today are allergic to everything. In the future, ours wars shall include peanuts and gluten as weapons of mass destruction.

Camping is confusing to me. You are basically paying to pretend to be homeless.

Life is uncertain. Every morning before I leave, I hug the kids and whisper, "avenge me" just in case.

Do the deaf think people are constantly screaming when they yawn?

My grandparents' zombies didn't run. They walked. Uphill. In the snow. They ate what brains they could find, and they were thankful for them.

I may have had too many energy drinks to drink today. When I pee it sounds like chipmunks telling me to beat Justin Beiber with a starfish.

You know you are desperate for answers when you look on the second page of Google.

Today is one of those days when I know I'm not mentally qualified to carry a gun. On at least four occasions I've mumbled to myself, "I wish I had a gun right now"

I love putting on underwear fresh out of the dryer. They are warm and cozy, and it's fun to scan the Laundromat and guess whose they are.

I don't carry life insurance because I'm going out of this world the same way I came in, as a burden to my family.

I heard that people who talk to themselves tend to be extremely smart. Did you know that? Yes, I did.

I will soon be rolling out my support website for those addicted to the Internet. Check back regularly for the link.

A guest just asked if I ever dated a Canadian. I told her my Canadian girlfriend was so hot her milkshake brought all the boys to the 0.914 meters

Sorry I keep looking at your chest while you're talking. It's amazing, what is that, oak?

Is it annoying when people answer their own questions? Yes it is. Do I wish they would stop? You bet!

I hope you got your mother a nice box of wine for Mother's Day. Remember, you are the reason she drinks.
I hate it when people misspell obviuos words.

I hope Puerto Rico does become a state. But, we need two more for a total of 53. As a prime number, we will truly be "the United States of America indivisible". Let's get on that.

This sentence is true.
The previous update is false.

I was once diagnosed as being colorblind. I was shocked. It totally came out of the green.

During these tough political times, I remember the words of the great Dr. Martin Luther King Jr. "These are some great tacos".

So happy to finally be finishing up my degree in TV/VCR repair.

If you play a Justin Beiber song backwards, you hear messages from the devil. Even worse, if you play it forward you hear Justin Beiber.

Please do not read this sentence. Thank you for your cooperation.

Just tried ancestry.com. Apparently I'm half centaur.

I avoid people that use clichés like the plague.

Watching UP with the kids. The movie that proves your life's adventure begins after your wife finally dies.

Can we all agree that The Wizard of Oz is basically about two women fighting over a pair of shoes?

Please settle an argument. Is it pronounced caramel or caramel?

Just spent an hour trying to get my tongue off the frozen festivals pole.

I am not trying to be confrontational. But, I am in the mood to fight someone to the death today.

"Thanks to Rosetta Stone, I can now speak Japanese with my parents!" What kind of parents do you have that didn't bother to teach you to speak their language?

Is there anyone that doesn't automatically check to see if the handicap stall is available when using a public restroom?

I've noticed a lot of people get uncomfortable if jokes don't end like they potato.

I've been thinking a lot about this and I'm pretty sure Chewbacca is my favorite wookie.

My childhood was such a blur. I should have had better glasses.

Do you think vegetarian zombies go around moaning "Grains! Grains!"?

Lately I feel like I never finish anyth

I'm not being condescending. I'm too busy thinking about far more important things you couldn't possibly understand.

Tried to donate to the local blood drive today. The nurse got all snippy wanted to know where I got it all.

So many blood drives going on. I am organizing a urine drive. I've heard there is a shortage of P- and I want to do my part. Support you community P-ple.

I hate being bipolar. It's awesome!

Big weekend planned. My Star Trek club is going to dress up as Klingons and ambush some loser civil war re-enactors.

Hey cool guy at the bar! FYI, you didn't start the t-shirt and sports coat look. Frankenstein did.

Chinese food to go: $16.84. Gas to go get it: $1.62. Getting home and realizing they forgot one of your containers: Riceless.

Relationships are like fat people, most of them don't work out.

You can't hum while holding your nose. Try it.

Auto correct can go straight to He'll

When people try extra hard to cover the keypad as they enter their pin at the ATM, I always want to whisper, "I saw it" when they're done.
My neighbor knocked on my door at three in the morning! Can you believe that? Lucky for him I was still up playing my drums.

Keep reading, I got nothin.

Next time I'm on an elevator with four or more strangers, I'm going to turn around and say, "I'm sure you're wondering why I've gathered you all here."

My high school girlfriend got "uses her kids as her Facebook profile picture" fat.

Apparently somebody in Detroit gets stabbed every 52 seconds...I would hate to be that guy

Make any conversation awkward by pulling out and starting a stopwatch without saying why you're doing it.

Just saw someone at Wal-Mart use a full size twix bar to stir their coffee.

-Every so often, I try to fornicate a large word into conversation, even if I'm not sure what it means.

At last, the whole world has converted to metric, a major 1.609km-stone!

I was about to leave my girlfriend because she is too controlling but she said no... so we are still together.

Be nice to people on your way up so they won't get suspicious when you're rich and you invite them to your island to hunt them for sport.

Just how hairy was the dude who invented a shampoo called Head & Shoulders?

One time I snuck a whole rotisserie chicken into a movie, cause candy is for amateurs.

The amount of big words I use incorrectly to try and sound smart is stammering.

What's your favorite movie about both space and jamming?

I'm sorry I offended you with my common sense

If you play my workday backwards, it's actually a nice story about idiots getting less and less annoying.

I'm going to the gym now. Not bragging. Just want you to know where to send the ambulance.

May be time to get in shape. Halfway up this flight of stairs and I'm considering setting up base camp and trying again in the morning.

I can't stand it when people don't know the difference between your and you're. There so stupid.

I'm a simple person with a complicated mind.

I'm not insulting you, I'm describing you.

Shortest horror story ever: I begin tucking him into bed and he tells me, "daddy check for monsters under my bed." I look underneath for his amusement and see him, another him, under the bed, staring back at me quivering and whispering, "daddy, there's someone on my bed."

When someone says "he's a good guy once you get to know him". They really mean, "he's not pleasant to be around, but you'll get used to it"

Used to date a model but the pieces kept falling off.

I was recently diagnosed as bipolar. I didn't know if I should laugh or cry.

Whenever someone asks me to sign their cast, I always write: 'last warning, you have a week to get the money together.'

The Walking Dead reminds you that other people would still be your biggest problem even if most of them died.

If you ever hear me say that I missed you it's only because I have bad aim.

Got fired from Bath and Body Works. Apparently coming

up behind customers & whispering, "it puts the lotion in the basket," is frowned upon.

For years I thought the Hyundai Sonata. Korean classic music car.

I have two wonderful kids. We have three total.

My daughter is NOT spoiled, she always smells like that for some reason.

Sometimes I just sit and run my fingers through my girlfriend's hair. Its a nice way to let her know I love her and also that we're out of napkins.

My doctor cured me of being a hypochondriac by placing me on an aggressive treatment of something called placebos.

I'm just a simple man, spreading the message that you can use two pancakes to make a sandwich. Am I a prophet? That's for history to decide.

I have an inferiority complex about my superiority complex. I know I'm better than you, but I feel really bad about it.

Shoot for the moon. Even if you miss, you'll be really far away from me with your motivational nonsense.

Today I tried the whole Yahoo vs Google thing. I typed "Why is there." Yahoo gave me "Why is there fuzz on a tennis ball" and Google gave me "Why is there a drunk Chinese man doing push ups on my front lawn." Google wins yet again

What's another word for word?

Target is nothing more than Wal-Mart in a tuxedo t-shirt.

My grandmother is 65 and still doesn't need glasses. She drinks right out of the bottle.

Do I seem self-centered, or is it just me?

I know the alphabet but I don't know it in alphabetical order

Today's revelation..If you say, "beer can" with a British accent, you're also saying "bacon" with a Jamaican accent.

I'm not saying golf isn't a sport, but you have to do

paperwork while you play it.

Girl, I like you so much, I might even let you hold my phone....some day, while its locked

Little old ladies in wheelchairs with blankets over their legs aren't fooling me.... retired mermaids.

Took a date to Starbucks simply because I forgot her name.

Nowhere in the story does it say Humpy dumpy was an egg.

I am studying my Spanish textbook. A book hasn't given me this much trouble since Waldo decided to visit that barber pole factory.

My mother was so proud of my gold spelling bee metal, she had it bronzed.

Basically I'm paying the cable company $80 a month for background noise to accompany my lap top usage.

Maybe NASA would be further along if they hadn't spent so much of their budget on foam mattresses and freeze-dried ice cream
I got to get some sleep. I need to be well rested for my

attempt at world domination tomorrow. Don't worry most of you will be spared....I will be requiring servants

Anytime someone accuses me of loving the sound of my own voice I think, "This person sounds terrible. They probably want me to sing"

You know you're in the wrong part of town, when you start seeing pay phones...

The key to a successful marriage is to never go to bed angry at each other. My wife and I haven't slept in 7 years.

I bet the weather tomorrow is going to be something someone I don't care about is going to discuss with me.

Wal-Mart: Because going to Target requires a shower.

Most of the time the past tense of 'hate' is 'love'.

I would pay so much money to watch a T Rex try to eat corn on the cob

Whenever I get sad I just imagine a T-Rex trying to put a hat on.

My girlfriend is gorgeous, selfless, graceful, highly intelligent and looking over my shoulder as I type.

According to my neighbor's journal, I have "boundary issues."

When I was younger, I always used to feel like a man trapped in a woman's body. However, that all changed when I was born.

Just took a shower. You have no idea how hard it was to sneak that thing out of Home Depot

One of the great mysteries to me is the fact that a woman could pour hot wax on her legs, rip the hair out by the roots, and still be afraid of a spider.

On the 12th Day of Christmas my Facebook gave to me...12 fools I'm blocking, 11 friends just watching, 10 notifications, 9 status updates, 8 friends complaining, 7 stalkers stalking, 6 invitations, Fiiiiiiiiiiiive Photo taaaaggsssss, 4 game requests, 3 silly comments, 2 inbox messages & a weird guy who won't stop poking meeee! :-)

Sorry that offended you, I really didn't think you'd get it. You say, "I'm sorry," I hear "I surrender."

Don't make fun of fat kids; they have enough on their plate. I wish there was an observation deck at Wal-Mart.

Whenever there's an awkward silence, try whispering, "Did you forget your line?"

Don't go broke trying to look RICH....act your wage!

Whenever someone calls me ugly, I get super sad and hug them, because I know how tough life is for the visually impaired...

I heard that people who talk to themselves tend to be extremely smart.. Did you know that? Yes, I did know that

I washed the car with my son today. Worst.sponge.EVER.

This girl I met last week says she wants a guy who is 'funny and spontaneous', yet when I tap on the kitchen window uninvited late at night dressed as a clown it's all panic and screaming.

Of course the Dalai Lama's quotes are all uplifting and optimistic... he's never been married.
Today is International Women's Day. It was actually

supposed to be held yesterday but they took too long to get ready.

I really wish I knew why my real parents sent me to Earth without my superpowers.

Jessica Simpson has already taught her baby everything she knows.

I'm sure it's just a coincidence that pop music has gotten worse since we started picking our artists on singing shows.

Does your heart flutter and does time seem to slow down when you see him? You're having a stroke.

I find it ironic that the colors red, white, and blue represent freedom until they are flashing behind you...

I got food poisoning today. I don't know when I'll use it though.

No baby, that's not sweat! It's condensation, because I'm so cool!

It's not really such an "Easy-Bake" oven when you're trying to cook a pot roast. This is taking *forever*.

When I was little I didn't care about things like what to wear, my parents dressed me. Looking back at some of my old pictures, it's obvious that my parents didn't care either.

I don't know what your problem is, but I'll bet it's really hard to pronounce.

I have tonight off so if anyone's free let's go somewhere and look at our phones together.

Opening a gym that teaches power walking and door knocking. Going to call it Jehovah's Fitness.

Beauty and the Beast is my favorite story that teaches kids that if you're ugly, hold a girl against her will & she'll eventually love you.

FACT : If you walk your child around on a leash, I will bend down and bark at it.

Give a man a match and he will be warm for a minute. Light him on fire and he will be warm for the rest of his life.

When people go underwater in movies, I like to hold my breath and see if I would survive in that situation. I almost died watching Finding Nemo...

Whenever anyone asks me who I'm on the phone with I say "Jake, from State Farm".

Debt collectors calling you? They don't call ME anymore after I answer the phone "Homicide, Detective Smith speaking, please give me your full name and direct affiliation with the victim who's phone you've just called." Problem solved!

Whenever I'm bored I stop a stranger and ask, "where am I?" and whatever they say I runaway screaming "Hahaha I'm a genius! I can teleport!"

Why talk on the phone for 5 minutes when we can have the exact same conversation via text over the next 10 hours

Thinking about moving to Alabama just so I don't have to scroll through all those other states when I sign up for websites.

I can't stand girls with poor spelling and grammar. Not my typo girls

Kissing is strange to me. "Um I really like you so I'm going to taste the inside of your face for a little while."

Walked right by an ex-girlfriend today. Not on purpose, I just didn't recognize her with her mouth closed.

My brain is about as well organized as the Wal-Mart $5 DVD bin.

So there's a film where a man's wife is brutally murdered by a serial killer and his son his left physically disabled. In a twist of events the son is kidnapped and kept in a tank while his father chases the kidnapper thousands of miles with the help of a mentally challenged woman. Finding Nemo is quite the thriller...

The problem with the world today is that the smart people are full of doubts while the stupid ones are full of confidence.

Forgot to take my phone with me to the restroom today. It was terrible! On a side note, Febreze contains no CFCs which are harmful to the ozone layer.

If Apple made a car, would it have windows?

If you're behind someone at an ATM, let them know you're not a threat by gently kissing their neck.

On the outside, I may appear like an emotionless sarcastic jerk, but just like an onion, when you peel off more layers, you find the exact same thing every single time and you start crying.

Why do people ask, "What were you thinking?" Obviously I was thinking I was going to get away with it and not have to explain it.

I've been trying to work on how I'm always silently judging people. I got the judging part down. I just need to work on the silently part.

I wish I were in a gang, I never know what to do with my hands when taking pictures.

Driving would be much more entertaining if there were no yellow lights.

Every time I eat Chinese I feel like I weigh won ton.

I tried to change my password to Twilight. But there was an error saying it contained too many useless characters.

I missed the part where gangnam style went from being a joke to being real

I wish Wal-Mart had a 10 Teeth or more line.

I am constantly putting things where they don't belong, like the cereal in the fridge or my keys in the laundry or my faith in other people.

My favorite part of Instagram is seeing what people consider "good" pictures of themselves.

Politeness has become so rare, that some people mistake it for flirting.

I am thinking: The best part about this message is that by the time you've finished reading it you realize that there is absolutely no point to it

My son can now reach the light switches so don't come over my house unless you're really into raves or want to have a seizure.

The only difference between a collector and a hoarder is the station the show is on.

I got 99 problems. I can only find 2 of my dalmations

I have decided to leave my past behind me.. So If I owe you money..I'm sorry. but I've moved on.

I am just a regular guy, putting on my Capri pants 3/4 leg at a time

Oh, this is my stepladder. My...my real ladder left when I was only 5.

Every time you make a "your mom" joke, I call my mom to check. Most of you are liars

I want to be buried in a spring-loaded casket with loads of confetti. In the future, some archaeologist is going to have one awesome day at work...

I understand that scissors can beat paper, and I get how rock can beat scissors, but there's no way paper can beat rock. Paper is supposed to magically wrap around rock leaving it immobile? Why can't paper do this to scissors? Forget scissors, why can't paper do this to people? Why aren't sheets of notebook paper constantly suffocating students as they attempt to take notes in class?

Just started my new Time Traveling club....... all new members please note the next meeting is last Tuesday at 6.00pm

I'll tell you why, because paper can't beat anybody, a rock would tear it up in two seconds. When I play rock, paper, scissors, I always choose rock. Then when somebody claims to have beaten me with paper I can punch them in the face with my already clenched fist and say, "Oh Sorry, I thought paper would protect you."

Could any of my Amish fans please email me and let me know what I can do to appeal more to your demographic.

I don't believe in astrology; I'm a Sagittarius and we're skeptical.

I'm learning to speak Cuban. It's just like Spanish but with a lot less words for luxury items.

"I'm up for the Dustin Hoffman role in the musical of 'Rain Man'! "3 minutes till Wapner" is a great song!"

I'm sure the popularity of Facebook REALLY skyrocketed after the invention of the internet.

When my wife picks a restaurant that I don't like, I just say "oh yeah, that's where that really cute girl works". Problem solved.

Tip for getting out of jury duty: Begin every answer with "according to the prophecy..."

Predicting the words "Ranch Dressing" will appear somewhere in my autopsy findings.

Spent the morning at the farmers market carefully selecting fruits and vegetables to throw away next Saturday.

When I get in an elevator, before I press a button I look at everyone inside and say "Are you ready to take this to a whole new level?"

My doctor says each piece of bacon takes 9 minutes off your life... If my math is right, I should've died in 1781...

Basically anything you buy at the hardware store looks like you're getting ready to take hostages.

Every single person on the planet has the reflexes of a superhero if you start scrolling through their photos while holding their phone.

We only use 10% of our brain, imagine if we used the other 60%

Anyone that knows me knows I'm a Vampire freak. I'm thinking of starting a George Michael cover band called Wham!pire...any backers? "Bleedom!"

Summer is here and we just roasted our first Wookie on the grill. Not bad, but it did taste a little Chewy.

I can't stand it when people start something and don't fi

Had the best Stuffed Roasted Bald Eagle for Memorial Day ever and had a great gift exchange. I love the holidays.

I'm selling my old dream catcher on Craig's List. Some good stuff with Megan Fox and one where I show up unprepared for finals.

In the fruit world, pineapples seem like jerks.

Every time a new American Idol is crowned, there's one less Indian casino booking available for the Little River Band.

So I was attacking the Death Star when it hit me! " I need a computer that can target the exhaust hatch!" So, I told the boys at Microsoft, and BOOM! Windows 7 comes out, now I can blow up the Death Star without relying on the Force. My name is Luke Skywalker, and Windows 7 was MY idea.

Funniest thing I've heard in a while: So I get the fact that the third guy was excited when he realized it was Superman in the sky, but what were the first two thinking...It's a bird, It's a plane....uh duh...why do you act shocked by those? Must have really looked like a couple of idiots at the time.

My fantasy Curling team is doing awesome....take that fantasy football freaks.

My new restaurant is Boba Cafe...Featuring Boba Fetta Cheese, Java the Hut, Ham Solos, Buffalo X-Wings, Pie-Fighters, Steak Jar Jar, Obi-Won-Ton Soup..and a diet Yoda. It's Amadali-cious....

I´ve been playing so my Wii Tennis on the ship, the doctor told me I was getting a Wii-knee.

I've decided to start watching Girls Gone Wild videos in reverse. Just to pretend the girls gain some dignity, put their clothes on, go back to school, and make their parents proud.

"I'll stop the world and melt with you!" because ceasing the planet's rotation, would cause cataclysmic seismic activity

Coming up on the 1-month anniversary of the execution of Chemical Ali. I remember him from his early days when was Gaseous Clay.

I hate it when I accidentally use the same word too many times in a sentence accidentally.

Ice dancing is timeless. It feels like it will never end.

Two birds with one stone. Found my wallet and unclogged the toilet.

I only hope I live long enough to see an Olympic pairs figure skating gold medal routine that artistically reenacts the plot to the movie 'Weekend at Bernies'.

I may or may not be wearing a cape right now that I made out of a warm bed sheet while doing laundry...hint: I AM.

If you were a gladiator in the heyday of Rome, I bet the inefficiency and randomness of how events were organized and scheduled would just drive you up the wall. Just saying.

The letters T and G are very close to each other on a keyboard. This recently became all too apparent to me and consequently I will never be ending a work email with the phrase "Regards" again.

Why does Frosty the Snowman wear a scarf? To keep his neck warm?

I would say thank you, but I deserve that.

I think the mistake a lot of us make is thinking the state-appointed shrink is our friend.

I can't stand cheap people. It makes me real mad when someone says something like, "Hey, when are you going to pay me that $100 you owe me?" or "Do you have that $50 you borrowed?" Man, quit being so cheap!

Someone just called me gullible, not sure what that means but I believe about anything

When you wish upon a star, your dreams can come true. Unless it's really a meteorite hurling toward the Earth. Then you're in trouble no matter what you wish for. Unless it's death by meteor.

I don't date older women I cant even stand age spots on a banana

Did you ever realize lifesavers only work if you are diabetic?

Just figured out that AARP must stand for Always Ask for Reduced Prices

Does anyone else suddenly feel insanely insecure when someone incredibly attractive looks you in the eye?

I remember way too many small details about people so I have to act dumb sometimes so I don't freak them out.

I never run voluntarily so if you ever see me running you should start running too because something is coming.

I think the guy who invented ties was trying to commit suicide. Then, he saw himself in the mirror & thought,..."wait, this looks nice."

Girlfriend said last night "You treat our relationship like some kind of game!" Which unfortunately cost her 12 points and a chance at the bonus round.

It's Google's 15th birthday today. Typical fifteen year old. It's got an answer for everything.

Time machine jokes aren't funny, you guys. My great grandson dies in a time machine crash.

I can tell people are judgmental just by looking at them.

Does it disturb anyone else that "The Los Angeles Angels" baseball team translates directly to "The The Angels Angels"?

Someone clearly cared that Jimmy cracked corn enough to write a song about it.

I figure that "Honey Boo-Boo" show puts us about six months away from just laughing at homeless people on television.

Good news! My girlfriend is graduating high school. She's the first in our family to do so.

I feel like we really lowered our expectations of what constitutes magic when we began using it to describe markers

I wish people were like Internet videos and you could tap them lightly to see a clock of how much longer they're going to be talking.

Wouldn't it be awesome if MTV had a show called "16 and Applying to Colleges"?

When someone is murdered, they always investigate the spouse first. And that pretty much tells you everything you need to know about marriage.

If I'm ever on life support unplug me and then plug me back in again and see if that works.

You'd think Winnie the Pooh would've gotten that shirt in at least a medium.

Of course Bruce Willis is going to keep playing the same movie roles. You know what they say about old habits.

If watermelon exists why don't airmelon, firemelon & earthmelon exist? ......the elemelons.

Why are there so many commercials for toilet paper? Who is not buying it?

If you're happy and you know it, you're probably exhausting to be around.

I will not be satisfied until I see a car with one woman sticker and twelve cat stickers.

Two things I hate: 1) People who form negative opinions of celebrities based only on what they see or hear on TV. 2) Justin Bieber.

My ex said she left me because of my short attention span. Unbeknownst to her I actually...wow. That's a cool word right? Unbeknownst..

The phrase, "Don't take this the wrong way" has a zero percent success rate.

I was addicted to the Hokey Pokey but I turned myself around.

Oh No! I just realized that I´m still it from a game of tag in 1987.

I want to change my name on Facebook to "No One," so when I try to add people, it will say, "No One wants to be your friend."

Please don't say you just had a newborn baby. If you say you just had a baby, the newborn part is assumed. Nobody thinks you just had a 12 year old.

Today I sent out a text saying, "Hey, I lost my phone, will you call it?" 12 people called me...I need smarter friends.

Did you know that dolphins are so smart that within a few weeks of captivity, they can train people to stand on the very edge of the pool and throw them fish?

Facebook asks what I'm thinking. Twitter asks what I'm doing. Foursquare asks where I am. The Internet has turned into a crazy girlfriend.

Ten years from now, one of the hardest challenges our kids will face will be finding a username that's still available.

We do get grumpy people at our show. So, if the person on your left is smiling, and the person on your right is smiling, guess who the grumpy one is.

5 out of 3 people can't even do simple fractions.

Sometimes I like to go to the hardware store and run around with a screwdriver shouting, "Ladies and gentlemen, this is not a drill!"

If people winked in real life as much as they do in texts, the world would be a really creepy place.

The tooth fairy teaches children that they can sell body parts for money

At what point did we start laughing and rolling on the floor when we read something funny?

The kid next door challenged me to a water balloon fight. I'm just waiting for the water to boil.

The first word I want to teach my kid is "brains". Then, until he/she learns another word, I'll have the cutest little zombie ever!

A cop just knocked on my door and told me that my dogs were chasing people on bikes. My dogs don't even own bikes...

Fun way to make someone self-conscious. Comment, "you are so brave" on all their selfies.

My girlfriend say the best part about being a girl, is she hasn't had to pay for alcohol since she was 8.

Not to say your kid is a brat, but I just saw an Oompa Loompa blow into a pitch pipe.

'WHO ORDERED 157 POUNDS OF SADNESS?!" - my way of introducing myself on a first date.

Sorry just got your text. Do you still need to go to the hospital?

I went to a vegan restaurant once. Wait, no, that was just a florist.

How does Disney decide who needs pants and who doesn't?

Not to brag but my bank says I have an outstanding balance.

If I had to describe myself in one word, it would be "doesn't understand directions."

I really want to rent a hot air balloon. Or at least a moderately attractive air balloon with a great personality.

You can tell yourself that Sesame Street is educational but Cookie Monster has lived there for like 40yrs and still can't conjugate verbs.

I was asked to leave Olive Garden because I kept saying "pasta la vista, baby" to people.

It would make more sense to put a teacher in every gun shop.

If you ask an undercover cop what the hills are alive with, he legally has to say "the sound of music" or else it's von trappment

"Lucy, in the sky, with diamonds." - John Lennon, the world's worst Clue player.

I think Groupon is crazy. If I had laser hair, I would never get it removed.

I hit a deer last night. It died instantly. I feel awful, but when I'm jogging I'm in my own world

Ever since I watched Jurassic Park. I check every shaving cream can for dinosaur embryos.

When someone asks for a glass of water, tell them, "Take a pitcher, it'll last longer."

Just ruined my pants sitting on a tomato I mistook for a tiny beanbag chair.

I'm not trying to start any trouble, but in that show "Full House" they could have fit more people in that house.

Why do people try to trick babies into thinking airplanes are delicious?

A cool way to insult someone: always use finger quotes when saying their name.

I can almost always tell if a movie doesn't use real dinosaurs.

Everyone who signed my middle school yearbook will be happy to hear that I have, in fact, stayed cool.

My friend wanted to feel like a princess for her wedding day, so I made her marry a man she never met in order to secure a French alliance.

Still feel bad for not considering that Dr. Pepper might be a woman.

While we are on the subject of Dr. Pepper. Who exactly is Mr. Pibb? We know Dr. Pepper at least took the time and effort to go on to grad school. What about this Pibb character? We know nothing. Maybe he is just riding Pepper's coat tails.

Just listened to the radio for an hour & I've concluded that all pop music is just someone auto tuning a 15 year old girl's text messages.

The average wife of Paul McCartney has 1.667 legs.

Yogurt? I didn't spend thousands of dollars on your proper education for you to use slang. It's "hellogurt"

Well, well, well. Guess who the grocery store asked to come back soon.

Not to brag, but I do have the record for the largest collection of air guitars.

Taking pictures with an iPad is the new fanny pack.

Burger King's full name was Burger Luther King Jr.

"Not Waldo, Not Waldo, Not Waldo, Not Waldo, Not Waldo, Not Waldo, Not Waldo, Not Waldo, Waldo, Not Waldo" --Where's Waldo audiobook

My dog licked the crumbs out of my computer keyboard and wrote the next Twilight book.

I would kill to win a Nobel Peace Prize.

I would seriously give my right arm to be ambidextrous

It's all fun and games until someone loses an eye, and then it's fun and games without depth perception.

I met three older women at our show that looked really scared and confused. Apparently, Vanessa, the driver, had a problem confusing state route signs with the speed limit. All the way across route 44, she kept the car below 44 mph, the constant honking from other cars was relentless. Everything was fine on route 65 into Branson. The real trouble started when they merged onto 165.

My wife and I decided to go with old-fashioned names for the twins. We have a son named Hunter and a daughter named Gatherer.

My good friend from the Philippines married one of our dancers from Holland. They are anticipating the birth of their first little Hallo-peano.

My Grandmother always used to say, "Trying is the first step toward failure." She said she never saw anyone try as hard as I did.

Grandma used to say I was like I was telepathetic. She had an accent though, so the "tele" was silent.

I don't cut women in half. I usually end up with the half that talks.
Grandma used to say that low self-esteem was normal in losers like me.

I remember the night Grandpa told my Grandma he lost her in a poker game. She screamed, "How could you do that?" He said, "It wasn't easy, I had to fold with four aces."

The neighbor told my Grandpa he was a horrible man to be around and if she had married him, she would poison his coffee. I remember him looking her straight in the eye and saying, "If I was married to you, I would drink it!"

I always thought Chanukah was the child of Han Solo and Chewbacca. Imagine my surprise.

You strike me as someone whose life is a nonstop series of bad decisions.

That was like the Munchkins on a camping trip, short and in tents.

So proud I'm about to finish my first novel...Christine by Stephen King

I have three children, so glad to finally have one of each.

I'm going to quote page 3 paragraph 7 word 13, "the".

I don't call use the term "redneck", I call them, "country music stars".

Grandma never needed glasses, she always drank right from the bottle.

I can't forget to get mom a mother's day gift. After all, she did change my diapers for the first 12 years of my life.

It's like the silent g in gnome, k in knife or the silent p in Jacuzzi.

This band is "bandtastic".
After watching you dance, I can't help but be envious of how your parents never taught you shame.

One sip of our specialty drink and you'll know how it tastes.

Ah ha, the foot is on the other hand now.

When I was a kid I had a free lemonade stand. However, the antidote was $20.

The answer to last night's trivia was.

I intend to live forever, so far so good.

1/2 this game is 90% mental.

I used to think you could stop time by thinking about pineapples.

For a month, I thought I had the best-behaved newborn baby ever. The baby didn't cry at all. My pride was shattered when I realized baby monitors have volume control.

When my Grandma retired, she started walking 5 miles a day. That was four years ago, we have no idea where she is today.

I'm going to have to go back to my old job as a bouncer at a day care.

I once got reprimanded for leaving the kids in the car while I ran into the post office. I learned my lesson. Now I make sure to get them out and put them in the trunk before I go in.

My twins are not fraternal, they are the other type called nocturnal, because they are always up all night. That's why daddy works on cruise ships.

Yes ladies, I am married, I finally I found just the right woman that needed to become a citizen.

This sunscreen SPF thing is getting out of control. If it goes much higher, when you open the can a sweatshirt and a hat are just going to fall out.

Whenever I go for a job interview, I open with, "I'm a bit of a germaphobe so please excuse me if I don't kiss you on the lips."

A great magician never revealed their secrets lucky for you, I'm not a great magician.

All I want is to not want anything

I'm suffering from Insania. It's sort of like Insomnia, only it's the voices in my head that can't sleep.

The pope quit, a meteor fell on Russia, an asteroid came close to earth, there's snow in Arizona, Star Wars and Star Trek have the same director! Who is playing Jumanji?!

Just remember the only thing standing between you and your dreams is your talent

Is it annoying when people answer their own questions? Yes it is. Do I wish they would stop? Absolutely.

I wonder what "don't touch" is in Braille.
What's Forrest Gump's password? 1forest1

Oh, you lost your phone and it's on silent? That's too bad. If you liked it then you should've put a ring on it.

On a scale of Doopers, you're pretty Super.

I only have two rules: 1. Be kind 2. If it jiggles when you move, cover it up

Of course it's you. If it was me I wouldn't even bring it up.

I'd save a lot more money on car insurance if they quit spending billions on advertising.

I'm a responsible person. People are always saying, "I know you're responsible for this."

One thing I learned from Star Wars is that inside a Tantan it's always "Luke" warm.

My parents surprised me with a truck. When I turned 16, but I got out of the way.

On career day, my teachers always laughed at me when I said I wanted to be a comedian after high school. They harassed me about what college I could possibly attend to get such a skill. Well here I am, a professional comedian, and NO ONE laughs at me now.

I've come up with the slow drivers I'm always stuck behind, "Slomosapians".

My memory is so good, I don't even remember the last time I forgot something.

I always wanted to buy a parrot and teach them to say, "Help! I've been turned into a parrot." As a magician, this would freak people out.

Some day, I want a son named Simon. I'm going to teach him to speak in third person about himself. "Simon says...".

I only trust people that like big butts. Apparently, they cannot lie.

Every time you make a typos, the errorists win.

I try not to plan my days ahead of time. Because, then the term "premeditated" gets thrown around the courtroom.

Was out last night and the woman in front of me bent over while I was dancing. The look she gave me when I started dancing up behind her was wicked. How I was supposed to know she just dropped an earring? And that no one else in the Starbucks could hear my iPod?

I was in a college band called 1023Mb. We never could get a gig.

I swear girls can be so ungrateful sometimes. I made her breakfast in bed, and instead of saying "thank you", she's all like..."how did you get in my house?"

If you think you are having a bad day...just remember somebody has Snooki as a mom.

Finally achieved my lifelong goal of having as many Tour de France titles as Lance Armstrong.

I just saw this girl texting and driving. I got so mad that I rolled down my window and threw my beer can at her car.

Taking the kids to see their grandparents for the holidays. I'm going to get a big fat candy cane, suck on it until it's pointy enough to stab someone, then let my son hold it as we walk through airport security. Is TSA willing to take candy from a baby? We will know soon enough.

I hate when I'm trying to be handsome and a more handsome man stands next to me and handsomes much harder than I can.

My first instinct when I see an animal is to say hello...My first instinct when I see a person is to avoid eye contact and hope it goes away.

College is incredibly depressing and didn't leave me much money. Since I couldn't afford anti-depressants. I started drinking the No More Tears shampoo before each class.

I have the best seat for the Justin Bieber concert! I'm at home, on my sofa, where I can't hear Justin Bieber.

When my mother was pregnant with me, she said she was high on life. She got busted for possession of life with the intent to distribute.

If I ever save anyone's life, I'm going to pull out my phone and say, "the subject is safe, the time is <blank> and the year is <blank>." Then I'm going to look them in the eye and say, "your future great great great grandson is a very important man" and just take off running.

Ambiguity: What happens in vagueness stays in vagueness.

I only read the constitution for the articles.

I'm starting group meetings at my house for people with OCD. Not because I have it, but because it's a great way to get your house cleaned for free.

I'm actually not funny. I'm just really mean and people think I'm joking.

When you say "I seen," I assume you won't finish that sentence with "the inside of a book."

Ladies, if a man says he will fix it, he will. There is no need to remind him every 6 months about it.

If I was an evil wizard, my horcrux would be the artificial heart in a sick child. Your move, Harry Potter.

I like to post WANTED DEAD OR ALIVE posters around town for Schrodinger's Cat.

Next time a stranger talks to me, when I'm alone, I will look at them shocked and just whisper quietly "You can see me?"

My mom used to tell me the ice cream truck only played music when it was sold out.

I tried to open a Mexican restaurant. It didn't go well. I don't want to taco bout it.

It's not that diabetes, heart disease and obesity runs in your family. It's that no one runs in your family.

Misuse of literally makes me figuratively insane.

I don't let my kids watch our show. Too much sax and violins.

Adult Truths:

1. I think part of a best friend's job should be to immediately clear your computer history if you die.

2. Nothing is worse than that moment during an argument when you realize you're wrong.

3. I totally take back all those times I didn't want to nap when I was younger.

4. There is great need for a sarcasm font.

5. How are you supposed to fold a fitted sheet?

6. Was learning cursive really necessary?

7. Map Quest really needs to start their directions on # 5. I'm pretty sure I know how to get out of my neighborhood.

8. Obituaries would be a lot more interesting if they told you how the person died.

9. I can't remember the last time I wasn't at least kind of tired.

10. Bad decisions make good stories.

11. You never know when it will strike, but there comes a moment at work when you know that you just aren't going to do anything productive for the rest of the day.

12. Can we all just agree to ignore whatever comes after Blue Ray? I don't want to have to restart my collection...again.

13. I'm always slightly terrified when I exit out of Word and it asks me if I want to save any changes to my ten-page document that I swear I did not make any changes

to.

14. I keep some people's phone numbers in my phone just so I know not to answer when they call.

15. I think the freezer deserves a light as well.

16. I have a hard time deciphering the fine line between boredom and hunger.

17. How many times is it appropriate to say "What?" before you just nod and smile because you still didn't hear or understand a word they said?

18. I love the sense of camaraderie when an entire line of cars team up to prevent a jerk from cutting in at the front. Stay strong, brothers and sisters!

19. Shirts get dirty. Underwear gets dirty. Pants? Pants never get dirty, and you can wear them forever.

20. Sometimes I'll look down at my watch 3 consecutive times and still not know what time it is.

From Branson, With L.O.L.

Christopher James

Branson, Missouri, USA

A man dies and appears at the Pearly Gates. "Have you ever done a good deed?" asks St. Peter.

"Sure, one time I came across a gang of bikers who were threatening a woman," the man says. "I walked up to the leader and punched him the face, kicked over his bike, and told him, " You leave her alone, or you'll answer to me."

"That was very brave of you," says St. Peter. "When did this happen?"

"About five minutes ago."

———

A blonde who's having financial troubles decides to kidnap a child for ransom. She writes on a piece of paper: "I've kidnapped your son. Leave $10,000 behind the oak tree in the park tomorrow at 7 AM. The blonde." She walks over to the park, grabs a little boy, pins the note to his jacket and tells him to run home.

The next morning, the blonde goes back to the park, where she sees the boy standing behind the oak tree.

"I'm supposed to give you this," he says, handing her a brown bag. As she counts the money, she notices a new note pinned to his jacket: "For the records, I can't believe that one blonde would do this to another."

———

A man is feeling depressed and decides to see a psychiatrist. He gets to the office, lies down on the couch, and tells the doctor his life story.

"I know exactly what your problem is," says the psychiatrist. "It's a simple matter of low self-esteem."

"Oh," says the man, dejected.

"Don't worry," says the doctor. "It's very common among losers like you."

━━━━━━━━━━━━━━━━━━━━━━━━━━━━━

An elderly man lying on his deathbed catches a whiff of homemade chocolate chip cookies wafting up the stairs. He gathers his strength and makes his way down to the kitchen. Just as he's reaching for the plate of cookies, his wife suddenly smacks him on the hand with a wooden spoon.

"Stay out of those," she yells. "They're for the funeral!"

━━━━━━━━━━━━━━━━━━━━━━━━━━━━━

On his first day at a new job, a guy attempts to phone an intern. "Bring me a cup of coffee pronto," he bellows.

"Do you know who you're talking to?" the voice on the other end of the line shouts back. "This is the president of the company!"

"Do you know who YOU are taking to, buddy?" the guy yells.

"No, I don't," replies the president.

"Thank goodness for that!"

━━━━━━━━━━━━━━━━━━━━━━━━━━━━━

"I've found a great job," a man says to his wife. "A 10 AM start, a 6 PM finish, no overtime, no weekends, and it pays $2,000 a week in cash."

"That's unbelievable," says the wife.

"I know, "says the husband. "You start Monday."

A man approaches a beautiful woman in a supermarket.

"I've lost my girlfriend," he tells her. "Can you stand here and talk to me for a few minutes?"

"Sure, but I don't understand how that would help," she replies.

"Well, every time I talk to a beautiful woman like you, my girlfriend appears out of nowhere."

Doctors say I have a multiple personality, but we don't agree with that.

"I have some good news and I have some bad news," says the doctor.

"OK," says the patient. "Give me the good news first."

"Well," says the doctor, "they're going to name a disease after you..."

A redneck is walking down the road one day when he sees his cousin coming toward him carrying a gunnysack.

"Hey there, Billy Ray," says the redneck. "Whatcha got?"

"Some chickens," replies the cousin.

"If I kin guess how many you got, kin I have one?"

"Shoot, if you guess right, I'll give you both of 'em."

"OK...Five."

Little Amy is in her backyard filling a big hole with dirt, occasionally smacking it down with her shovel. Her curious neighbor peers over the fence. "What are you doing there, Amy?" he asks.

"I'm...I'm burying my goldfish, "she replies tearfully.

"Oh, sorry," he says, "but isn't that an awfully big hole for a goldfish?"

Amy pats down the last heap of earth, looks up, and says, "That's because he's inside your stupid cat!"

"I knew I had a problem with dyslexia the day I went to a toga party dressed as a goat."

A Frenchman with a parrot perched on his shoulder walks into a bar. The bartender says, "Wow, that's really neat! Where did you get him?"

"In France," the parrot replies. "They've got millions of 'em."

A burglar breaks into a house one night and turn on his flashlight to find an expensive stereo. As he approaches it, a voice behind him whispers, "Jesus is watching you."

The startled burglar turns and shines his light on a caged parrot in the corner of the room.

"Was that you?" asks the burglar.

"Yes," answers the parrot. "My name is Moses. How do you do? Squawk!"

Amused at the talking bird, the burglar laughingly asks, "What kind of people name a parrot Moses?"

"Squawk! The same kind of people who name a Rottweiler Jesus."

Dear Son:

I'm writing this slow cause I know you can't read fast.

We don't live where we did when you left. Your Dad read in the paper where most accidents happen within twenty miles of the house, so we moved. This place has a washing machine. The first day I put four shirts in it, pulled the chain, and haven't seen them since.

It's only rained twice this week. Three days the first time and four days the second time.

The coat you wanted me to send, your Aunt Sue said was too heavy to mail with all those big buttons on it so we cut them off and they're in the pockets.

We got a bill from the funeral home, said if we didn't make the last payment on Grandma's funeral, up she comes.

Your Uncle Joe fell in the whisky vat yesterday -- some men tried to pull him out but he fought 'em all off and finally drowned. We cremated him right after and he's still burning good this morning.

Three of your friends went off the bridge in a pick-up truck, one was driving, two in the back. The driver rolled the window down and swam out. The two in the back couldn't get the tailgate open so they drowned too.

Not much news this time, nothing much happens round here, will try to write more next time.

Love, Your Mama

P.S. Was gonna send you some money but already had this sealed up.

A blonde goes into the doctor's office and says that her body hurts wherever she touches it.

"That's odd, "says the doctor. "Show me what you mean."

The woman touches her elbow and screams in agony. She then touches her knee and screams, and then pushes on her ankle and screams.

"Just as I thought," says the doctor. "You have a broken finger."

Q: Why did the blonde plant Cheerios in her garden?

A: She thought they were donut seeds.

Two men are fishing on a riverbank when they see a funeral procession passing by. One of the men stands up, takes off his hat, and bows.

"That was a very nice thing to do," says the second man.

"Well," says the first, "we were married for 25 years."

"I've been told we only use 10% of our brains, imagine if we could learn to use the other 60%."

A redhead, a brunette, and a blonde are in a bar when the bartender tells them about a magic mirror in the ladies' room. Apparently, he says, the mirror gives rewards if you stare into it and say something true. But if you lie, you're sucked into the mirror and never heard from again.

So the redhead heads to the bathroom, looks into the mirror, and says, "I think I'm the most beautiful woman in this bar." A million dollars suddenly appears before her.

Then the brunette heads into the bathroom, looks into the mirror, and says, "I think I'm the smartest woman in this bar." The key to a new Ferrari materializes in her fingers.

Then the blonde goes in, looks into the mirror, and begins, "I think..." And she's sucked in and never heard from again.

A guy hears a knock at his door. When he answers it, there's nobody there, but there's a snail on the welcome mat. Frustrated, the guy picks up the snail and hurls it into the street.

Five years go by, and there's another knock at the door. The man answers it, and again there's no one standing there. But there's a snail on the welcome mat. The snail looks up and says, "What was that all about?"

Alcohol and calculus don't mix.
Never drink and derive.

Two guys decide to go bungee jumping in Mexico. Having never seen bungee jumping before, a crowd of locals gathers to watch. The first guy jumps and when he bounces back up, he's got cuts and bruises all over his face. The second guy helps him back onto the bridge. "What happened," he says. "Was the cord too long?"

"The cord was fine," he gasps, "It was the crowd. What's a piñata?"

My Grandmother once reflected that she wishes she could go back in time when...

-Decisions were made by going "eeny-meeny-miney-mo."

-Mistakes were corrected by simply exclaiming, "do over!"

-"Race issue" meant arguing about who ran the fastest.

- Money issues were handled by whoever was the banker in "Monopoly."

-Catching the fireflies could happily occupy an entire evening.

-It wasn't odd to have two or three "best friends."

-Being old referred to anyone over 20.

-The net on a tennis court was the perfect height to play volleyball and rules didn't matter.

-It was magic when dad would "remove" his thumb.

-It was unbelievable that dodge ball wasn't an Olympic event.

-Having a weapon in school meant being caught with a slingshot.

-Scrapes and bruises were kissed and made better.

-It was a big deal to finally be tall enough to ride the "big people" rides at the amusement park.

-Getting a foot of snow was a dream come true.

-Abilities were discovered because of a "double-dog-dare."

-Saturday morning cartoons weren't 30-minute ads for action figures.

-"Oly-oly-oxen-free" made perfect sense.

-Spinning around, getting dizzy and falling down was cause for giggles.

-The worst embarrassment was being picked last for a team.

-War was a card game.

-Water balloons were the ultimate weapon.

-Baseball cards in the spokes transformed any bike into a motorcycle.

-Taking drugs meant orange-flavored chewable aspirin.

A wife sees a daytime talk show where they're discussing remarriage after a spouse passes away. After chatting with her mother and friends about it at length, she asks her husband later that night in bed, "Honey, if I were to die, would you remarry?"

He replies, "Well, after a considerable period of grieving and maybe even therapy...we all need companionship. So, I guess I would."

Spurred on by her husband's response, she then asks, "If I died and you remarried, would you let the woman live in this house?"

He replies, "We've spent a lot of money getting this house just the way we want it. It seems like a waste to give it all up...so, yes, I guess I would."

Looking flustered, the wife finally asks, "Would you let her use my golf clubs?"

"Oh no...she's left handed."

It's October, and an Indian chief thinks it's going to be a cold winter. So he instructs his tribe to collect wood.

To double-check his prediction, the chief calls the National Weather Service and asks a meteorologist if the winter is going to be a cold one.

The man responds, "According to our indicators, we think it might."

So the chief tells his people to find extra wood, just in case. A week later he calls the National Weather Service again, and they confirm that a harsh winter is headed their way.

The chief orders all his people to scavenge every scrap of wood they can. Two weeks later he calls the National Weather Service again and asks, "Are you absolutely sure this winter is going to be very cold?"

"Absolutely," the man replies. "The Indians are collecting wood like crazy."

"He who laughs last thinks slowest."

This guy runs home and bursts in yelling, "Pack your bags, honey. I just won the lottery!"

She says, "Oh, wonderful! Should I pack for the beach or the mountains?"

He replies, "I don't care...just get out!"

"I can't stand it when people start something and don't fi

A ventriloquist is touring clubs in Florida. With his dummy on his knee, he's going through his usual dumb blonde jokes when a blonde woman in the audience stands on her chair and shouts, "I've heard enough of your stupid blonde jokes. What does the color of a person's hair have to do with her worth as a human being? It's guys like you who keep women like me from being respected at work, and from reaching our full potential!"

The embarrassed ventriloquist starts to apologize, when the blonde yells, "You stay out of this, mister! I'm talking to that little guy sittin' on your knee!"

Be nice to your kids. They'll choose your nursing home.

A brother and sister are talking to each other when the little boy gets up and walks over to his grandfather. "Make a frog noise, Grandpa," he says.

"Why?" asks the grandfather.

"Please, please make a frog noise," pleads the boy.

"Not unless you tell me why."

"Because Mommy said when you croak we can all go to Disneyworld."

Always remember you're unique, just like everyone else.

Brian gets a parrot for his birthday. It has a bad attitude and a worse vocabulary. Every other word is offensive. Brian tries to change the bird's behavior with polite words, soft music...but nothing works. Out of desperation, he throws the bird in the freezer. It squawks, kicks, screams, and then falls silent. Brian, worried, swings the freezer door open. The parrot calmly steps out. "I believe I may have offended you with my rude language and actions. I will endeavor at once to correct my behavior."

Brian is amazed at the change in the bird's attitude and is about to ask what caused it when the parrot continues, "May I ask what the chicken did?"

―――――――――――――――――――――――――

A woman goes into a funeral home to make arrangements for her husband. She tells the director she'd like him to be buried in a dark blue suit.

"Wouldn't it be easier to bury him in the black suit he is wearing?" he asks. But she insists on dark blue and gives him a blank check to buy one with.

The woman returns for the wake later that day and sees her husband in the coffin wearing a dark blue suit.

"It's beautiful, " she says. "How much did it cost?"

"Nothing," says the director. "After you left, a corpse with a blue suit was brought in. They were about the same size so I asked his widow if she would mind if her husband was buried in a black suit. She said fine, so...I switched the heads."

―――――――――――――――――――――――――

A genii offers to grant a man one wish.

"Build me a bridge to Hawaii, " says the man, "so I can drive over anytime."

The genii says, "Think of the logistics of that kind of undertaking. The supports to reach to the bottom of the Pacific. The concrete and steel it would take. I can do this, of course, but it's hard for me to justify your desire for worldly things. Take a little time and think of another wish."

The man thinks for a while and says, "I wish I could understand women."

After a moment, the genii says, "You want two lanes or four?"

———————————————————————————

A little man walks into a biker bar and clears his throat. "Um, which of you gentlemen owns the Doberman tied to the parking meter?"

A big biker turns slowly on his stool, "It's mine. Why?"

"Well," squeaks the little man, "I believe my dog just killed it."

"What?" bellows the biker in disbelief. "What kind of dog you got than can take down my Doberman?"

"Sir," answers the little man meekly, "it's a Chihuahua."

"A Chihuahua! A Chihuahua?" shouts the biker. "How could a little Chihuahua kill a Doberman?"

"Well, it appears that he choked on it, sir."

———————————————————————————

Three guys die in a car crash and meet St. Peter.

"When you're in your casket and your friends and family are gathered around, what would you like to hear them say?" St. Peter asks.

"I'd like to hear someone say I made a difference," answers the first guy.

"I'd like to hear someone say I was a good family man, " answers the second guy.

"And you?" St. Peter asks the third guy.

"I guess I'd like to hear someone say, 'Look! He's moving!'"

Radio conversation released by the chief of naval operations 10.10.95...

Americans: Please divert your course 15 degrees to the north to avoid a collision.

Canadians: Recommend you divert YOUR course 15 degrees to the south to avoid a collision.

Americans: This is the captain of a US Navy ship. I say again, divert YOUR course.

Canadians: No, I say again divert YOUR course.

Americans: THIS IS THE AIRCRAFT CARRIER USS ENTERPRISE; WE ARE A LARGE WARSHIP OF THE US NAVY. DIVERT YOUR COURSE NOW.

Canadians: This is Rocky Point Lighthouse. Your call.

Farmer Joe is suing a trucking company over injuries he suffered in an auto accident. The company's layer begins to cross-examine the plaintiff.

"Isn't it true you said, 'I'm fine,' at the scene of the accident?" asks the lawyer.

"Well, I'll tell you what happened," farmer Joes starts.

"Did you or did you not say, 'I'm fine!'" thunders the lawyer.

"Let me explain," pleads the farmer. "I had just loaded my mule Daisy into the trailer and was driving down the highway when this semi-truck crashed into us. I was hurt real bad. When the highway patrolman came on the scene, he heard Daisy moaning and groaning. He took one look at her, pulled out his gun, and shot her between the eyes.

Then he came across the road with his gun in hand, looked at me, and said, "Your mule was in such bad shape I had to shoot her. How are you?"

"I've been thinking about this a lot lately, and I'm pretty sure my favorite Wookie is Chewbacca."

An elderly man in Miami calls his son, Dave, in New York and says, "I hate to ruin your day, but your mother and I are divorcing. Forty years of misery is enough! I'm sick of her, and I'm sick of talking about this so call your sister in Chicago and tell her," and then hangs up.

The son frantically calls his sister, who goes nuts upon hearing the news.

She calls her father and yells, "You are NOT getting a divorce! Dave and I will be there tomorrow. Until then, don't do a single thing, do you hear me?"

The father hangs up the phone, turns to his wife, and says, "It worked! The kids are coming for a visit, and they are paying their own way!"

A man walks into a bar, sits down and orders a drink. He says "Give me a drink before problems start!" The bartender doesn't understand but gives the man a drink.

After 15 minutes the man orders a drink again saying "Give me a drink before problems start!" The bartender looks a little bit confused but pours the man a drink.

This goes on the whole night and after the 15th drink the bartender is totally confused and asks the man "What do you mean with before problems start? And when are you going to pay for all the drinks you drunk."

The man answers "You see, now the problems start!"

Two friends get lost during a hiking trip through the desert. Several days later, they are dehydrated and near death.

Out of nowhere, they see a tree in the distance that appears to be covered with bacon. One guy sprints ahead, only to be gunned down in a hail of gunfire.

"Run!" the dying man yells out. "It's not a bacon tree. It's a ham bush!"

Q: How many psychiatrists does it take to change a light bulb?

A: One, but the bulb has got to want to change itself.

A guy walks into the doctor's office with a banana stuck in one ear, a cucumber in the other and a strawberry wedged in his nostrils.

"Doc, I need help," says the guy. "Something's wrong with me."

"Well," says the doctor, "I can see you're not eating right."

"I hate it when I accidentally use the same word too many times in a sentence accidentally."

A man takes his Rottweiler to the veterinarian and says, "My dog is going cross-eyed. Is there anything you can do to help him?"

"Well," replies the vet, "let's have a look at him." So he picks up the dog and checks its eyes.

After a quick exam, the vet turns to the owner and says, "I'm afraid I'm going to have to put him down."

"Why? Just because he's cross-eyed?"

"No," says the vet, "It's just that he's really heavy!"

Actual Call Center Calls

Customer: "I've been calling 700-1000 for two days and can't get through; can you help?"
Operator: "Where did you get that number, sir?"
Customer: "It's on the door of your business."
Operator: "Sir, those are the hours that we're open."

Caller: "Can you give me the telephone number for Jack?"
Operator: "I'm sorry, sir, I don't understand who you are talking about."
Caller: "On page 1, section 5, of the user guide it clearly states that I need to unplug the fax machine from the AC wall socket and telephone Jack before cleaning. Now, can you give me the number for Jack?"

Operator: "I think it means the telephone plug on the wall."

Directory Enquiries
Caller: "I'd like the number of the Argo Fish Bar, please."
Operator: "I'm sorry, there's no listing. Are you sure that the spelling is correct?"
Caller: "Well, it used to be called the Bargo Fish Bar but the 'B' fell off."

Then there was the caller who asked for a knitwear company in Woven.
Operator: "Woven? Are you sure?"
Caller: "Yes. That's what it says on the label -- Woven in Scotland. "

On another occasion, a man making heavy breathing sounds from a phone box told a worried operator: "I haven't got a pen, so I'm steaming up the window to write the number on."

Tech Support: "I need you to right-click on the Open Desktop."
Customer: "OK."
Tech Support: "Did you get a pop-up menu?"
Customer: "No."
Tech Support: "OK. Right-Click again. Do you see a pop-up menu?"
Customer: "No."
Tech Support: "OK, sir. Can you tell me what you

have done up until this point?"

Customer: "Sure. You told me to write 'click' and I wrote 'click'."

Tech Support: "OK. At the bottom left hand side of your screen, can you see the 'OK' button displayed?"

Customer: "Wow! How can you see my screen from there?"

Tech Support: "OK, the computer should be telling you to press any key."

Customer: ....

Tech Support: "Let me know when you are ready to move on."

Customer: "I keep looking and looking and I can't find the "any key"."

Tech Support: "Now, to install the program, we need to insert the CD."

Customer: "And where do I do that?"

Tech Support: "The CD drive in the front of your computer, push the eject button and the tray should open."

Customer: "CD player? I've been using that as a cup holder!"

Tech Support: "Press the left button on your computer mouse to continue."

Customer: "I'm trying but my toe won't reach."

Tech Support: "Your toe?"

Customer; "Yes, I thought you used the mouse like my sewing machine peddle, am I doing it wrong?"

A blonde walks into a library, goes up to the front desk, and says, "I'm here to see the doctor."

"This is a library, dearie," says the librarian.

"Oh, I'm sorry," whispers the blonde. "I'm here to see the doctor."

A married couple is walking past their neighbors' house. "Dave and Linda are so loving toward each other," says the wife. "Every time he sees her, he gives her a big kiss...unlike someone I know."

"Hey, I'd love to," says the husband. "But I don't know her that well."

Did you hear about the dyslexic agnostic insomniac?

He stayed awake all night wondering if there really was a dog.

A man and a woman were having dinner in a fine restaurant. Their waitress, taking another order at a table a few paces away, noticed that the man was slowly sliding down his chair and under the table, with the woman acting unconcerned.

The waitress watched as the man slid all the way down his chair and out of sight under the table. Still, the woman dining across from him appeared calm and unruffled, apparently unaware that her dining companion had disappeared.

After the waitress finished taking the order, she came over to the table and said to the woman, "Pardon me, ma'am, but I think your husband just slid under the table."

The woman calmly looked up at her and replied firmly, "No he didn't. He just walked in the door."

―――――――――――――――――――――――――

ATTORNEY: She had three children, right?
WITNESS: Yes.
ATTORNEY: How many were boys?
WITNESS: None.
ATTORNEY: Were there any girls?

ATTORNEY: How was your first marriage terminated?
WITNESS: By death.
ATTORNEY: And by whose death was it terminated?

ATTORNEY: Can you describe the individual?
WITNESS: He was about medium height and had a beard.
ATTORNEY: Was this a male or a female?

ATTORNEY: Is your appearance here this morning pursuant to a deposition notice which I sent to your attorney?

WITNESS: No, this is how I dress when I go to work.

ATTORNEY: ALL your responses MUST be oral, OK? What school did you go to?

WITNESS: Oral.

A blonde is on a date with a geography teacher. "Believe it or not, I know all the state capitals," she says proudly.

"Oh, yeah?" says the guy. "What's the capital of Wisconsin?"

"That's easy," she replies. "It's a W."

A general is giving the president his daily briefing. He concludes by saying: "Yesterday, 3 Brazilian soldiers were killed in an accident"

"OH NO!" the President exclaims. "That's terrible!"

His staff sits stunned at this display of emotion, nervously watching as the President sits, head in hands. Finally he looks up and asks.......... "How many is a Brazillion??!'

"I hate it when people misspell obviuos words."

Sherlock Holmes and Dr. Watson go on a camping trip, set up their tent, and fall asleep. Some hours later, Holmes wakes his faithful friend.

"Watson, look up at the sky and tell me what you see."

Watson replies, "I see millions of stars."

"What does that tell you?"

Watson ponders for a minute. "Astronomically speaking, it tells me that there are millions of galaxies and potentially billions of planets. Astrologically, it tells me that Saturn is in Leo. Time wise, it appears to be approximately a quarter past three. Theologically, it's evident the Lord is all-powerful and we are small and insignificant. Meteorologically, it seems we will have a beautiful day tomorrow. What does it tell you?"

Holmes is silent for a moment, and then speaks. "Watson, you idiot, someone has stolen our tent."

Q: What do you call a musician without a girlfriend?

A: Homeless.

Q: Where's the English Channel?

A: I don't know - our television doesn't pick it up.

Life lessons from my Grandfather

1. Trouble in marriage often starts when a man gets so busy earnin' his salt that he forgets his sugar.

2. Too many couples marry for better, or for worse, but not for good.

3. When a man marries a woman, they become one; but the trouble starts when they try to decide which one.

4. If a man has enough horse sense to treat his wife like a thoroughbred, she will never turn into a nag.

5. On anniversaries, the wise husband always forgets the past - but never the present.

6. The bonds of matrimony are a good investment only when the interest is kept up.

7. Many girls like to marry a military man - he can cook, sew, and make beds and is in good health, and he's already used to taking orders.

8. Eventually you will reach a point when you stop lying about your age and start bragging about it.

9. The older we get, the fewer things seem worth waiting in line for.

10. Some people try to turn back their odometers. Not me, I want people to know "why" I look this way. I've traveled a long way and some of the roads weren't paved.

11. How old would you be if you didn't know how old you are?

12. I don't know how I got over the hill without getting to the top.

13. One things no one tells you about aging is that it is such a nice change from being young.

14. Ah, being young is beautiful, but being old is comfortable.

15. Old age is when former classmates are so gray and wrinkled and bald, they don't recognize you.

16. If you don't learn to laugh at trouble, you won't have anything to laugh at when you are old.

Two guys are in a bar.

First one: "My wife is an angel."

Second one: "You're lucky! Mine is still alive."

An English teacher wrote the words, "Woman without her man is nothing" on the blackboard and asked the students to punctuate it so that it made sense.

The boys wrote: "Woman, without her man, is nothing."

The girls wrote: "Woman! Without her, man is nothing."

Just before Thanksgiving Jim and Eddie are out hunting for turkeys when Jim keels over and collapses. He doesn't seem to be breathing and his eyes are glazed. Eddie gets out his cell phone and calls the emergency services.

He gasps, "My friend Jim is dead! What can I do?"

The operator says, "Calm down, I can help. First, let's make sure he's dead."

There's a silence, then a shot is heard.

Back on the phone, Eddie says, "OK, now what?"

A man follows a woman with a parrot out of a movie theater. He stops her and says, "I'm sorry to bother you, but I couldn't help but notice that your bird seemed to understand the movie. He cried at the right spots, he was fidgeting in his seat during the boring parts, and he laughed at the jokes. Don't you find that unusual?"

"I do indeed," she replies. "He hated the book."

One day a teacher was giving a lecture on philosophy, and had the class enthralled. It was a brilliant lecture.

Suddenly, over his head a bright light flashed and a genii appeared and approached the teacher.

She said, "You are doing such a good job teaching this class, I have decided to give you one wish. You can have infinite money, infinite wisdom, or infinite knowledge."

Thinking for a minute, he humbly asked for infinite wisdom. She tapped him with a magic wand and disappeared in a flash. The class came forward to hear the first words from a man with infinite wisdom.

He said, "It would have been wiser to take the money..."

A man tells his doctor he's unable to do all the things around the house that he used to do. After the exam, he says, "Now, doc, I can take it. Tell me in plain English what is wrong with me."

"In layman's terms, you're lazy," says the doctor.

"Ok, now give me a medical term, so I can tell my wife."

Charles Dickens walks into a bar and orders a Martini.

The bartender says "Olive or Twist?"

A foolproof method for sculpting an elephant: get a huge block of marble, and then chip away everything that doesn't look like an elephant.

Grandma reflects on living in the 60s VS. being over 60

Then: Long hair.

Now: Longing for hair.

Then: Moving to California because it's cool.

Now: Moving to California because it's warm.

Then: Trying to look like Marlon Brando or Elizabeth Taylor.

Now: Trying not to look like Marlon Brando or Elizabeth Taylor.

Then: Getting out to a new, hip joint.

Now: Getting a new hip joint.

Then: Rolling Stones.

Now: Kidney stones.

Then: Peace sign.

Now: Mercedes logo.

Then: Passing the driver's test.

Now: Passing the vision test.

Then: "Whatever"

Now: "Depends"

A man returns from Africa feeling very ill. He visits his doctor, who immediately rushes the guy to the Mayo Clinic.

The man wakes up to the ringing of a telephone in a stark room at the hospital and answers it. "We've received the results from your tests," says the doctor on the other end of the line. "Bad news, you have Ebola."

"Oh, my," cries the man. "Doc! What am I going to do?""

"Don't' worry. First, we're going to put you on a diet of pizza, pancakes, and pita bread." Says the doctor.

"Will that cure me?"

"No, but it's the only food we'll be able to get under the door."

Bacon and Eggs walk into a bar...

The bartender says "Sorry, we don't serve breakfast."

A frog telephones the Psychic Hotline and is told, "You're going to meet a beautiful young girl who will want to know everything about you."

The frog says, "This is great! Will I meet her at a party or what?"

"No," says the psychic, "next term in her biology lesson."

———————————————————————

A passenger train is creeping along, slowly. Finally it creaks to a halt. A passenger sees a conductor walking by outside. "What's going on?" she yells out the window. "Cow on the track!" replies the conductor.

Ten minutes later the train resumes its slow pace. Within five minutes, however, it stops again. The woman sees the same conductor walk again.

She leans out the window and yells, "What happened? Did we catch up with the cow again?"

———————————————————————

An artist asked the gallery owner if there had been any interest in his paintings on display at that time.

"I have good news and bad news," the owner replied, "the good news is that a gentleman enquired about your work and wondered if it would appreciate in value after your death.

When I told him it would, he bought all 15 of your paintings."

"That's wonderful," the artist exclaimed, "what's the bad news?"

"The guy was your doctor..."

———————————————————————

A businessman enters a tavern, sits down at the bar, and orders a double martini on the rocks.

After he finishes the drink, he peeks inside his shirt pocket, and orders another double martini. After he finishes that one, he peeks inside his shirt pocket again and orders yet another double martini.

The bartender says, "Look, buddy, I'll bring ya' martinis all night long - but you gotta tell me why you look inside your shirt pocket before you order a refill."

The customer replies, "I'm peeking at a photo of my wife. When she starts to look good, I know it's time to go home."

———————————————————————

Two guys are talking while sitting on a bench in the park. "All of my ancestors followed the medical profession." said the first.

"Doctors?" queried the second.

"Nope. Undertakers and lawyers."

———————————————————————

The new employee stood before the paper shredder looking confused.

"Need some help?" a secretary, walking by, asked.

"Yes," he replied, "how does this thing work?"

"Simple," she said, taking the fat report from his hand and feeding it into the shredder.

"Thanks, but where do the copies come out?"

Q: What is the difference between a Southern zoo and a Northern Zoo?

A: At Southern Zoos the animal descriptions include cooking times.

There were two men in a building site. One of them said, "Can you help me find my ear?"

The other one, holding up an ear, asked, "Is this it?"

"No" replied the first one, "mine has a pencil behind it."

Humor in Church

Q. *What kind of man was Boaz before he married Ruth?*

A. Ruthless.

Q. What do they call pastors in Germany?

A. German Shepherds.

Q. *Who was the greatest financier in the Bible?*

A. *Noah. He was floating his stock while everyone else was in liquidation.*

Q. Who was the greatest female financier in the Bible?

A. Pharaoh's daughter. She went down to the bank of the Nile and drew out a little prophet.

Q. What kind of motor vehicles are in the Bible?

A. Jehovah drove Adam and Eve out of the Garden in a Fury. David's Triumph was heard throughout the land. Also, probably a Honda, because the apostles were all in one Accord.

Q. *Who was the greatest comedian in the Bible?*

A. Samson. He brought the house down.

Q. What excuse did Adam give to his children as to why he no longer lived in Eden ?

A. Your mother ate us out of house and home.

Q. Which servant of God was the most flagrant law breaker in the Bible?

A. Moses. He broke all 10 commandments at once.

Q. Which area of Palestine was especially wealthy?

A. The area around Jordan. The banks were always overflowing.

Q. Who is the greatest babysitter mentioned in the Bible?

A. David. He rocked Goliath to a very deep sleep.

Q. Which Bible character had no parents?

A. Joshua, son of Nun.

Q. Why didn't they play cards on the Ark?

A. Because Noah was standing on the deck.

Did you know it's a sin for a woman to make coffee? Yup, it's in the Bible. It says. . 'He-brews'

There were two men in a building site. One of them said, "Can you help me find my ear?"

The other one, holding up an ear, asked, "Is this it?"

"No" replied the first, "mine has a pencil behind it."

Q: How many visitors to an art gallery does it take to change a light bulb?

A: Two. One to do it, and one to say "Huh! My four-year old could've done that!"

"If there are any idiots in the room, will they please stand up," said the sarcastic teacher. After a long silence, one freshman rose to his feet.

"Now then, mister, why do you consider yourself an idiot?" enquired the teacher with a sneer.

"Well, actually I don't," said the student, "but I hate to see you standing up there all by yourself."

Christopher Columbus was the best deal-maker in history. He left not knowing where he was going, and upon arriving, not knowing where he was. He returned not knowing where he had been, and did it all on borrowed money.

A worker was called to the office by his supervisor for talking back to his foreman.

Supervisor: "Is it true that you called him a liar?"

Worker: "Yes, I did."

Supervisor: "Did you call him stupid?"

Worker: "Yes."

Supervisor: "And did you call him an opinionated, bullheaded egomaniac?"

Worker: "No, but would you write that down so I can remember it?"

A bald man took a seat in a beauty shop. "How can I help you?" asked the stylist.

"I went for a hair transplant," the guy explained, "but I couldn't stand the pain. If you can make my hair look like yours without causing me any discomfort, I'll pay you $5000."

"No problem," said the stylist and she quickly shaved her head.

A man walks into a bar, sits down and says to the girl next to him, "Hey, you want to hear a great blonde joke?"

"Listen, buddy," the girl replies. "You can surely tell that I AM blonde. My two friends here are both world ranked judo masters and they're blonde too. Now, do you still want to tell that joke?"

"Nah," the man replies, "I don't feel like explaining it three times."

Two cannibals are eating a clown. One says to the other, "Hey, does this taste funny to you?"

A cop pulls over a couple for speeding. He walks up to the driver and says, "I clocked you doing 80 mph, sir."

"Gee, officer," says the driver, "I had it on cruise control at 60."

"Don't be silly, dear," the wife chimes in. "This car doesn't have cruise control."

As the cop begins to write the ticket, the husband growls to his wife, "Can't you just keep your mouth shut?"

The wife smiles and says, "You should be happy the radar detector went off when it did."

"A radar detector, eh?" says the officer. "Those are illegal in this state." He starts to write up a second ticket.

"Will you please keep your mouth shut!" screams the husband to the wife.

The officer bends down, looks at the woman and asks, "Does he always talk to you like that?"

"Oh, heavens no," she replies, "Only when he's been drinking."

Two elderly couples are playing bridge, and at one point the wives go into the kitchen. One of the gentlemen says, "Last night we went to a really fantastic restaurant. I highly recommend it."

"What is the name of it?" the other man asks.

The first man thinks for a while and finally says, "Hey, what's the name of that flower? You know, it's red and has thorns on its stem."

"You mean a rose?"

"Yeah, that's it." He turns toward the kitchen and yells, "Rose, what's the name of that restaurant we went to last night?"

A man joins a Tibetan temple. He takes a vow of silence but is allowed to say two words every year.

After a long 12 months of eating rice, sleeping on a wooden bed with an old blanket, and working 14 hours a day in the fields, the man goes to the head monk and says, "More blankets."

Another year passes, and he visits the head monk and says, "More food."

The man goes through one more year eating good meals and sleeping well, but he's drained by the long workdays. He calls on the head monk uses his two words to say, "I'm leaving."

"Good," the head monk replies. "You've done nothing but complain since you got here."

Late one night a guy is showing some friends around his brand new apartment.

The last stop is the bedroom, where a big brass gong sits next to the bed.

"What's that gong for?" the friend asks him.

"It's not a gong," the man replies, "It's a talking clock."

"How does it work?"

The guy picks up a hammer, gives the gong an ear shattering whack and steps back.

Suddenly, someone on the other side of the wall in the next apartment screams, "For goodness sake, you jerk...it's 3:30 in the morning!"

"What time does the library open?" the man on the phone asked.

"Nine A.M." came the reply. "And what's the idea of calling me at home in the middle of the night to ask a question like that?"

"Not until nine A.M.?" the man asked in a disappointed voice.

"No, not till nine A.M.!" the librarian said. "Why do you want to get in before nine A.M.?"

"Who said I wanted to get in?" the man sighed sadly. "I want to get out."

A man walks into a bar, and orders a drink. As he sits there, the jar of nuts on the bar tells him what a nice shirt he is wearing. Disturbed by this, he reaches for the pay phone. As he approaches the phone, it starts screaming and shouting at him.

He runs to the bar and explains this to the barman. The barman apologizes and says, "The peanuts are complimentary, but the pay phone is out of order!"

Signs that you have grown up

1. Dinner and a movie is the whole date instead of the beginning of one.

2. You actually eat breakfast food at breakfast time.

3. Eating a basket of chicken wings at 3 AM now severely upsets, rather than settles, your stomach.

4. 6:00 AM is when you get up, not when you go to bed.

5. You hear your favorite song on an elevator.

6. You watch the Weather Channel.

7. Your friends marry and divorce instead of date and break up.

8. You go from 130 days of vacation time to 14.

9. Jeans and a sweater no longer qualify as "dressed up".

10. You're the one calling the police because those kids next door won't turn down the stereo.

11. Your car insurance goes down and car payments go up.

12. You feed your dog Science Diet instead of McDonald's leftovers.

13. Sleeping on the couch makes your back hurt.

14. You no longer take naps from noon to 6 PM!

A lady inserted an 'ad' in the classifieds: "Husband wanted".

Next day she received a hundred letters. They all said the same thing: "You can have mine."

The village blacksmith finally found an apprentice willing to work hard at low pay for long hours. The blacksmith immediately began his instructions to the lad: "When I take the shoe out of the fire, I'll lay it on the anvil; and when I nod my head, you hit it with this hammer."

The apprentice did just as he was told. Now *he's* the village blacksmith.

Q: How many artists does it take to change a light bulb?

A: Ten. One to change it, and nine to reassure him about how good it looks.

A man speaks frantically into the phone, "My wife is pregnant, and her contractions are only two minutes apart!"

"Is this her first child?" the doctor queries.

"No, you idiot!" the man shouts. "This is her husband!"

———————————————————————

A housewife, an accountant and a lawyer were asked, "How much is 2+2?"

The housewife replies: "Four!"

The accountant says: "I think it's either 3 or 4. Let me run those figures through my spreadsheet one more time."

The lawyer pulls the drapes, dims the lights and asks in a hushed voice, "How much do you want it to be?"

———————————————————————

A woman and her little girl were visiting the grave of the little girl's grandmother. On their way through the cemetery back to the car, the little girl asked, "Mommy, do they ever bury two people in the same grave?"

"Of course not, dear." replied the mother, "Why would you think that?"

"The tombstone back there said 'Here lies a lawyer and an honest man.'"

———————————————————————

"Doctor, Doctor, You've got to help me - I just can't stop my hands shaking!"

"Do you drink a lot?"

"Not really - I spill most of it!"

An applicant was asked if he was familiar with any machines. He said "Four."

"That's great. What are the four machines?"

He said, "Coke, coffee, candy, and cigarette."

After surgery, the surgeon told his patient: "I'm afraid we're going to have to open you back up. Because, you see, I forgot my rubber gloves inside you."

Patient: "Well, if that's all, I'd rather pay for them if you just leave me alone."

Doctor: "I have some bad news and some very bad news."

Patient: "Well, you might as well give me the bad news first."

Doctor: "The lab called with your test results. They said you have 24 hours to live."

Patient: "24 hours! That's terrible!! What could be worse?! What's the very bad news?"

Doctor: "I've been trying to reach you since yesterday."

Ladies, when a woman steals your spouse, there is no better revenge than to let her keep them.

"Doctor" said the patient, "are you sure I'm suffering from pneumonia? I once heard of a doctor treating someone with pneumonia -- and finally he died of typhus."

"Don't worry, that won't happen to me", the doctor replied. "If I treat someone with pneumonia he'll die of pneumonia."

A guy walks into work, and both of his ears are all bandaged up. The boss says, "What happened to your ears?"

He says, "Yesterday I was ironing a shirt when the phone rang and pshhhhh! I accidentally answered the iron."

The boss says, "Well, that explains one ear, but what happened to your other ear?"

He says, "Well, jeez, then I had to call the doctor!"

The woman applying for work in a Florida lemon grove seemed way too qualified for the job.

Foreman: "Look Miss, have you any actual experience in picking lemons?"

Woman: "Well, as a matter of fact, yes! I've been divorced three times."

Dear Christopher,

I know you joke about having A.D.D. so I thought I would email you about a condition I call A. A. A. D. D. - Age Activated Attention Deficit Disorder

This is how it manifests:

I decide to water my garden. As I turn on the hose in the driveway, I look over at my dirty ol' Pontiac and decide it needs washing. As I start toward the garage, I notice that there is mail on the porch table that I brought up from the mailbox earlier. I decide to go through the mail before I wash the car. I lay the car keys down on the table, put the junk mail in the garbage can under the table, and notice that the can is full. So, I decide to put the bills back on the table and take out the garbage first. But then I think, since I'm going to be near the mailbox when I take out the garbage anyway, I may as well pay the bills first. I take my checkbook off the table, and see that there is only one check left. My extra checks are in my desk in the study, so I go inside the house to my desk where I find the can of Diet Coke that I had been drinking. I'm going to look for my checks, but first I need to push the Diet Coke aside so that I don't accidentally knock it over. I see that the pop is getting warm, and I decide I should put it in the refrigerator to keep it cold. As I head toward the kitchen with the Diet Coke, a vase of flowers on the counter catches my eye--they need to be watered. I set the Diet Coke down on the counter, and I discover my reading glasses that I've been searching for all morning. I decide I better put them back on my desk, but first I'm going to water the flowers. I set the glasses back down on the counter, fill a container with water and suddenly I spot the TV remote. Someone left it on the kitchen table. I realize that tonight when we go to watch TV, I will be looking for the remote, but I won't remember that it's on the kitchen table, so I decide to put it back in the den where it belongs, but first I'll water the flowers. I pour some water in the flowers, but quite a bit of it spills on the floor. So, I set the remote back down on the table, get some towels and wipe up the spill. Then I head down the hall trying to remember what I was planning to do.

At the end of the day:
* the car isn't washed
* the bills aren't paid

there is a warm can of Diet Coke sitting on the counter

the flowers don't have enough water

there is still only one check in my check book

I can't find the remote

I can't find my glasses

I don't remember what I did with the car keys.

Then when I try to figure out why nothing got done today, I'm really baffled because I know I was busy all day long, and I'm really tired. I realize this is a serious problem, and I'll try to get some help for it, but first I'll send Christopher an e-mail.

After a quarrel, a husband said to his wife, "You know, I was a fool when I married you."

She replied, "Yes, dear, but I was in love and didn't notice."

Man is incomplete until he is married. Then he is finished.

A woman was telling her friend, "It is I who made my husband a millionaire."

"And what was he before you married him?" her friend asked.

"A billionaire" she replied.

The young lady, upon her engagement, went to her mother and said, "I've found a man just like father!"

Her mother replied, "So what do you want from me, sympathy?"

A little boy asked his father "Daddy, how much does it cost to get married?"

And the father replied, "I don't know son, I'm still paying."

I want to die in my sleep like my grandfather...not screaming and yelling like the passengers in his car...

Young Son: "Is it true, Dad, I heard that in some parts of Africa a man doesn't know his wife until he marries her?"

Father: "That happens in every country, son."

"I never knew what real happiness was until I got married; and then it was too late."

Q. What's the difference between a run over dog and a run over lawyer?

A. The dog has skid marks before it.

A tourist asks a man in uniform, "Are you a policeman?"

"No, I am an undercover detective."

"So why are you in uniform?"

"Today is my day off."

The most effective way to remember your wife's birthday is to forget it once.

Teacher: "If you reached in your right pocket and found a nickel, and you reached in your left pocket and found another one, what would you have?"

Boy: "Somebody else's pants."

A policeman pulls a man over for speeding and asks him to get out of the car. After looking the man over he says "Sir, I couldn't help but notice your eyes are bloodshot. Have you been drinking?"

The man gets really indignant and says, "Officer, I couldn't help but notice your eyes are glazed. Have you been eating doughnuts?"

A policeman stops a lady and asks for her license.

Policeman: "Lady, it says here that you should be wearing glasses."

Woman: "Well, I have contacts."

Policeman: "I don't care who you know! You're still getting a ticket!"

One evening a man arrived home from work and found his wife waiting for him at the front door.

"I want you to take me somewhere expensive tonight," she said.

"No problem, honey," the man replied. " I know just the place."

"So," his wife asked as they were pulling out of their driveway, "where are we going?"

"The gas station," he replied.

A woman's husband had been slipping in and out of a coma for several months, but she dutifully stayed by his bedside every single day. One afternoon, he finally opened his eyes. When he did, he looked at his wife and said, "You've always been with me through the bad times. When I got fired, you were there to support me. When my business failed, you were there. When I got hot, you were by my side. When we lost the house, you stayed with me, and when my health started failing, you were still by my side. So you know what?"

"What dear?" his wife asked, smiling bravely.

"I think you're really bad luck," he said.

A husband and wife were dining out together when the wife noticed that her husband kept staring at an attractive woman who was sitting at the bar throwing back drink after drink.

"Do you know that woman?" she asked.

"Yes," her husband replied. "She's an ex-girlfriend. She started drinking after we broke up, and apparently she hasn't been sober since."

"My goodness!" his wife exclaimed. "Who'd have thought a person could celebrate for that long?"

"Dad, can you write in the dark?"

"I think so. What is it you want me to write?"

"Your name on this report card."

Where in the nursery rhyme does say that Humpty Dumpty is an egg?

Wisdom From My Grandmother

1. If you're too open minded, your brains will fall out.

2. Age is a very high price to pay for maturity.

3. Going to church doesn't make you a Christian any more than going to a garage makes you a mechanic.

4. Artificial intelligence is no match for natural stupidity.

5. If you must choose between two evils, pick the one you've never tried before.

6. My idea of housework is to sweep the room with a glance.

7. Not one shred of evidence supports the notion that life is serious.

8. It is easier to get forgiveness than permission.

9. For every action, there is an equal and opposite government program.

10. If you look like your passport picture, you probably need the trip.

11. Bills travel through the mail at twice the speed of checks.

12. A conscience is what hurts when all your other parts feel so good.

13. Eat well, stay fit, and die anyway.

14. Men are from earth. Women are from earth. Deal with it.

15. No husband has ever been shot while doing the dishes.

16. A balanced diet is a cookie in each hand.

17. Middle age is when broadness of the mind and narrowness of the waist change places.

18. Opportunities always look bigger going than coming.

19. Junk is something you've kept for years and throw away three weeks before you need it.

20. There is always one more imbecile than you counted on.

21. Experience is a wonderful thing. It enables you to recognize a mistake when you make it again.

22. By the time you can make ends meet, they move the ends.

23. Thou shalt not weigh more than thy refrigerator.

24. Blessed are they who can laugh at themselves for they shall never cease to be amused.

Teacher: "Johnny, what is the outside of a tree called?"

Johnny: "I don't know."

Teacher: "Bark, Johnny, bark!"

Johnny: "Woof, woof..!"

So ya know, I've been taking these kung-fu classes lately. I must say they're great. They teach you how to be as powerful as a tiger, as quick as a monkey, and as smart as a dragon. Just the other day, these guys came up to me with a knife and demanded money. So, I turned into a chicken and ran!

A man wrote a letter to a small hotel he planned to visit on his vacation: "I would very much like to bring my dog with me. He is well groomed and very well behaved. Would you be willing to permit me to keep him in my room with me at night?"

An immediate reply came from the hotel owner, who said, "I've been operating this hotel for many years. In all that time, I've never had a dog steal towels, bedclothes, silverware or pictures off the walls. I've never had to evict a dog in the middle of the night for being disorderly. And I've never had a dog run out on a hotel bill. Yes, indeed, your dog is welcome at my hotel. And, if your dog will vouch for you, you're welcome to stay here, too."

A busload of tourists arrives at Runnymede. They gather around the guide who says, "This is the spot where the barons forced King John to sign the Magna Carta."

A fellow at the front of the crowd asks, "When did that happen?"

"1215," answers the guide.

The man looks at his watch and says, "Darn! Just missed it by a half hour!"

Teacher: "You know you can't sleep in my class."

Boy: "I know. But maybe if you were just a little quieter, I could."

A man on his deathbead made one final dying request of his wife.

"Darling, promise me you will marry Andrew after I'm gone," he said.

"Of course, honey, anything you want," his wife replied, "but I thought you hated Andrew."

With his last dying breath her husband said, "I do."

How do you make a blonde laugh on Saturday?
Tell her a joke on Wednesday.

The child comes home from his first day at school.
Mother: "What did you learn today?"
Kid: "Not enough. I have to go back tomorrow."

A guy stood over his tee shot for what seemed an eternity, looking up, looking down, measuring the distance, figuring the wind direction and speed. Driving his partner nuts.

Finally his exasperated partner says, "What is taking so long? Hit the ball!"

The guy answers, "My wife is up there watching me from the clubhouse. I want to make this a perfect shot."

"Well, you don't stand a chance of hitting her from here!"

A brunette is trying to get across a river and suddenly she spots a blonde on the other side.

She yells over to the blonde, "Hey, excuse me! How do I get over to the other side?"

After a quick survey of the river, the blonde calls back, "You ARE on the other side!"

An English professor complained to the pet shop proprietor, "The parrot I purchased uses improper language."

"I'm surprised," said the owner. "I've never taught that bird to swear."

"Oh, it isn't that," explained the professor. "But yesterday I heard him split an infinitive."

Two boll weevils grew up in South Carolina. One went to Hollywood and became a famous actor. The other stayed behind in the cotton fields and never amounted to much.

The second one, naturally, became known as the lesser of the two weevils.

Four People

This is a story about four people, named Everybody, Somebody, Anybody, and Nobody.

There was an important job to be done, and Everybody was sure that Somebody would do it.

Anybody could have done it, but Nobody did. Somebody got angry about this, because it was Everybody's job. Everybody thought Anybody could do it, but Nobody realized that Everybody wouldn't do it. It ended up that Everybody blamed Somebody when Nobody did what Anybody could have done!

Knowing that the minister was very fond of cherry brandy, one of the church elders offered to present him with a bottle on one condition... that the Pastor acknowledges receipt of the gift in the church paper.

"Gladly," replied the good man.

When the church magazine came out a few days later, the elder turned at once to the "appreciation" column. There he read: "The minister extends his thanks to Elder Brown for his gift of fruit and for the spirit in which it was given."

I would give my right arm
to be ambidextrous.

Top 45 Oxymorons

45. Act naturally

44. Found missing

43. Resident alien

42. Advanced BASIC

41. Genuine imitation

40. Airline Food

39. Good grief

38. Same difference

37. Almost exactly

36. Government organization

35. Sanitary landfill

34. Alone together

33. Legally drunk

32. Silent scream

31. Living dead

30. Small crowd

29. Business ethics

28. Soft rock

27. Butt Head

26. Military Intelligence

25. Software documentation

24. New classic

23. Sweet sorrow

22. Childproof

21. "Now, then ..."

20. Synthetic natural gas

19. Passive aggression

18. Taped live

17. Clearly misunderstood

16. Peace force

15. Extinct Life

14. Temporary tax increase

13. Computer jock

12. Plastic glasses

11. Terribly pleased

10. Computer security

9. Political science

8. Tight slacks

7. Definite maybe

6. Pretty ugly

5. Twelve-ounce pound cake

4. Diet ice cream

3. Working vacation

2. Exact estimate

1. Microsoft Works

A funeral service is being held for a woman who has just passed away. As the pallbearers are carrying out the casket, they accidentally bump into a wall. Hearing a faint moan from inside, the woman's husband opens the casket and finds that his wife is actually alive!

She dies again, 10 years later, at which point her husband has to go through another funeral. This time when the pallbearers carry the casket toward the door, the husband yells out, "Watch out for the wall!"

A couple drove several miles down a country road, not saying a word after an earlier discussion had led to an argument, and neither wanted to concede their position.

As they passed a barnyard of mules and pigs, the wife sarcastically asked, "Relatives of yours?"

"Yep," the husband replied, "In-laws."

Two old men in a retirement village were sitting in the reading room and one said to the other, "How do you really feel? I mean, you're 75 years old, how do you honestly feel?"

"Honestly, I feel like a newborn baby. I've got no hair, no teeth, and I just peed myself."

I wonder...

1. Why are there interstate highways in Hawaii?

2. What WAS the best thing before sliced bread?

3. What would chairs look like if our knees bent the other way?

4. If you choke a smurf, what color does it turn?

5. If you cross a four-leaf clover with poison ivy, would you get a rash of good luck?

6. What the world be like without theoretical questions?

7. If a no-armed man has a gun, is he armed?

8. If you got into a taxi and the driver starts driving backwards, does she/he owe you money?

9. If con is the opposite of pro, then is Congress the opposite of progress?

10. If you throw a cat out a car window, does it become kitty litter?

Three retirees, each with a hearing loss, were taking a walk one fine March day.

One remarked to the other, "Windy, ain't it?"

"No," the second man replied, "It's Thursday."

The third man chimed in, "So am I. Let's have a coke."

A man sitting through the first quarter of the Super Bowl can't help but notice the conspicuously vacant seat next to the man to the right of him.

Wanting to make polite conversation he leans over to the man and says "Can you believe someone paid all that money for a seat to the Super Bowl and then doesn't show up?"

The man turns to him and says, "That's my wife's seat she recently passed away." "Oh I am so sorry to hear that." the first man said, "didn't anyone else in your family want the ticket?"

The second man never took his eyes from the football game, "Sure, they did, but they're all at the funeral."

Grandchildren don't make a man feel old ... it's the thought that he's married to a grandmother.

I had trouble with the idea of turning 30 and was oversensitive to any signs of advancing age. When I found a prominent gray hair in my bangs, I pointed to my forehead and asked my husband, "Oh no, have you seen this?"

"What?" he asked. "The wrinkles?"

There's this guy who had been lost and walking in the desert for about 2 weeks. One hot day, he sees the home of a missionary. Tired and weak, he crawls up to the house and collapses on the doorstep. The missionary finds him and nurses him back to health. Feeling better, the man asks the missionary for directions to the nearest town.

On his way out the back door, he sees this horse. He goes back into the house and asks the missionary, "Could I borrow your horse and give it back when I reach the town?" The missionary says, "Sure but there is a special thing about this horse. You have to say 'Thank The Lord' to make it go and 'Amen' to make it stop."

Not paying much attention, the man says, "Sure, OK." So he gets on the horse and says, "Thank The Lord" and the horse starts walking. Then he says, "Thank The Lord, Thank The Lord" and the horse starts trotting. Feeling really brave, the man says, "Thank The Lord, Thank The Lord, Thank The Lord, Thank The Lord, Thank The Lord" and the horse just about takes off.

Pretty soon he sees this cliff coming up and he's doing everything he can to make the horse stop. "Whoa, stop, hold on!!!! "Finally he remembers, "Amen!!" and the horse skids to a stop 4 inches from the edge of the cliff.

The man sinks slowly back into the saddle, sighs deeply, and lets out a heartfelt, " Thank The Lord."

Why didn't the lifeguard rescue the drowning hippie?
She was too far out.

While strolling on the beach, a man finds a golden lamp. Rubbing the lamp, he is suddenly confronted by a genii.

"I shall grant you three wishes, but keep in mind, your ex wife shall receive double your wish."

The man thinks carefully and then proceeds to ask for one billion dollars.

"Your wish is granted, plus, your wife in now the recipient of TWO billion dollars."

"Unhappy about this situation, the man thinks carefully and asks to be granted an extra one hundred years of life."

"It is done, and your wife shall now live an additional TWO hundred years."

Frustrated, the man looks the genii straight in the face, "I want you to scare me half to death."

A retired man who volunteers to entertain patients in nursing homes and hospitals went to one local hospital in Brooklyn and took his portable keyboard along. He told some jokes and sang some funny songs at patients' bedsides.

When he finished he said, in farewell, "I hope you get better."

One elderly gentleman replied, "I hope you get better too."

"I hold an OCD meeting at my house every second Tuesday. I don't have OCD, it's just a way to get my house cleaned for free."

A blonde wanted to go ice fishing. She'd seen many books on the subject, and finally, after getting all the necessary tools together, she made for the ice. After positioning her comfy footstool, she started to make a circular cut in the ice. Suddenly, from the sky, a voice boomed,

"THERE ARE NO FISH UNDER THE ICE."

Startled, the blonde moved further down the ice, poured a thermos of cappuccino, and began to cut yet another hole. Again from the heavens the voice bellowed,

"THERE ARE NO FISH UNDER THE ICE."

The blonde, now worried, moved away, clear down to the opposite end of the ice. She set up her stool once more and tried again to cut her hole. The voice came once more,

"THERE ARE NO FISH UNDER THE ICE." She stopped, looked skyward, and said, "IS THAT YOU LORD?"

The voice replied, "No, this is the manager of the hockey rink."

A couple goes out to dinner to celebrate their 50th wedding anniversary.

On the way home, she notices a tear in his eye and asks if he's getting sentimental because they're celebrating 50 wonderful years together. He replies, "No, I was thinking about the time before we got married.

Your father threatened me with a shotgun and said he'd have me thrown in jail for 50 years if I didn't marry you. Tomorrow I would've been a free man!"

Two old men have been best friends for years, and they both live to their early 90's, when one of them suddenly falls deathly ill. His friend comes to visit him on his deathbed, and they're reminiscing about their long friendship, when the dying man's friend asks, "Listen, when you die, do me a favor. I want to know if there's baseball in heaven."

The dying man said, "We've been friends for years, this I'll do for you." And then he dies.

A couple days later, his surviving friend is sleeping when he hears his friend's voice. The voice says, "I've got some good news and some bad news. The good news is that there's baseball in heaven."

"What's the bad news?"

"You're pitching on Wednesday."

———————————————————————

Two old men are talking about their aches, pains and bodily functions.

One seventy-year-old man says, "I have this problem. I pee like clockwork at 7AM every morning."

The other old man says, "So what's your problem?"

"I don't wake up until nine."

———————————————————————

A wise old gentleman retired and purchased a modest home near a junior high school. He spent the first few weeks of his retirement in peace and contentment. Then a new school year began.

The very next afternoon three young boys, full of youthful, after-school enthusiasm, came down his street, beating merrily on every trashcan they encountered. The crashing percussion continued day after day, until finally the wise old man decided it was time to take some action.

The next afternoon, he walked out to meet the young percussionists as they banged their way down the street. Stopping them, he said, "You kids are a lot of fun. I like to see you express your exuberance like that. In fact, I used to do the same thing when I was your age. Will you do me a favor? I'll give you each a dollar if you'll promise to come around every day and do your thing."

The kids were elated and continued to do a bang-up job on the trashcans. After a few days, the old-timer greeted the kids again, but this time he had a sad smile on his face. "This recession's really putting a big dent in my income," he told them. "From now on, I'll only be able to pay you 50 cents to beat on the cans." The noisemakers were obviously displeased, but they accepted his offer and continued their afternoon ruckus. A few days later, the retiree approached them again as they drummed their way down the street.

"Look," he said, "I haven't received my Social Security check yet, so I'm not going to be able to give you more than 25 cents. Will that be okay?" "A lousy quarter?" the drum leader exclaimed. "If you think we're going to waste our time, beating these cans around for a quarter, you're nuts! No way, mister. We quit!" And the old man enjoyed peace.

━━━━━━━━━━━━━━━━━━━━━━━━━━━━━━━

A 60-year-old man went to a doctor for a check-up. The doctor told him, "You're in terrific shape. There's nothing wrong with you. Why, you might live forever; you have the body of a 35-year-old. By the way, how old was your father when he died?"

The 60-year-old responded, "Did I say he was dead?"

The doctor was surprised and asked, "How old is he and is he very active?"

The 60-year-old responded, "Well, he is 82 years old and he still goes skiing three times a season and surfing three times a week during the summer."

The doctor couldn't believe it. So, he asked, "Well, how old was your grandfather when he died?"

The paitient responded again, "Did I say he was dead?"

The doctor was astonished. He said, "You mean to tell me you are 60 years old and both your father and your grandfather are alive? Is your grandfather very active?"

The 60-year-old said, "He goes skiing at least once a season and surfing once a week during the summer. Not only that," said the patient, "my grandfather is 106 years old, and next week he is getting married again."

The doctor said, "At 106-years, why on earth would your grandfather want to get married?"

His patient looked up at the doctor and said, "Did I say he wanted to?"

"Give me a sentence about a public servant," said the Mother helping her son at home.

The small boy wrote: "The fireman came down the ladder pregnant."

The mother took her son aside to correct him. "Don't you know what pregnant means?" she asked.

"Sure," said the young boy confidently. "It means 'carrying a child.'"

An 80-year-old couple were having problems remembering things, so they decided to go to their doctor to get checked out to make sure nothing was wrong with them. When they arrived at the doctor's, they explained to the doctor about the problems they were having with their memory.

After checking the couple out, the doctor tells them that they were physically okay but might want to start writing things down and make notes to help them remember things. The couple thanked the doctor and left.

Later that night while watching TV, the old man got up from his chair and his wife asks, "Where are you going?"

He replies, "To the kitchen."

She asks, "Will you get me a bowl of ice cream?"

He replies, "Sure."

She then asks him, "Don't you think you should write it down so you can remember it?"

He says, "No, I can remember that."

She then says, "Well, I also would like some strawberries on top. You better write that down cause I know you'll forget."

He says, "I can remember that, you want a bowl of ice cream with strawberries."

She replies, "Well, I also would like whip cream on top. I know you will forget that so you better write it down."

Irritated, he says, "I don't need to write that down, I can remember that." He then fumes into the kitchen.

After about 20 minutes he returns from the kitchen and hands her a plate of bacon and eggs.

She stares at the plate for a moment and says, "You forgot my toast."

Two elderly women were out driving in a large car of which both could barely see over the dashboard. As they were cruising along they came to an intersection. The stoplight was red but they just went on through. The woman in the passenger seat thought to herself "I must be losing it, I could have sworn we just went through a red light."

After a few more minutes they came to another intersection and the light was red again and again they went right though. This time the woman in the passenger seat was almost sure that the light had been red but was really concerned that she was losing it. She was getting nervous and decided to pay very close attention to the road and the next intersection to see what was going on.

At the next intersection, sure enough, the light was definitely red and they went right through and she turned to the other woman and said, "Mildred! Did you know we just ran through three red lights in a row! You could have killed us!"

Mildred turned to her and said, "Oh, am I driving?"

A rabbi was called to a Miami Beach Nursing Home to perform a wedding.

An anxious old man met him at the door. The rabbi sat down to counsel the old man and asked several questions. "Do you love her?"

The old man replied, "I guess."

"Is she a good Jewish woman?"

"I don't know for sure," the old man answered.

"Does she have lots of money?" asked the rabbi.

"I doubt it."

"Then why are you marrying her?" the rabbi asked.

"She can drive at night," the old man said.

Three ladies were discussing the travails of getting older. One said, "Sometimes I catch myself with a jar of mayonnaise in my hand, while standing in front of the refrigerator, and I can't remember whether I need to put it away, or start making a sandwich."

The second lady chimed in with, "Yes, sometimes I find myself on the landing of the stairs and can't remember whether I was on my way up or on my way down."

The third one responded, "Well, ladies, I'm glad I don't have that problem. Knock on wood," as she rapped her knuckles on the table, and then said, "That must be the door, I'll get it!"

With the average cost for a Nursing Home per day reaching $188.00,there is a better way when we get old & feeble. I have already checked on reservations at the Holiday Inn for a combined long-term stay discount and senior discount of $49.23 per night. That leaves $138.77 a day for:

1. Breakfast, lunch and dinner in any restaurant I want, or room service.

2. Laundry, gratuities and special TV movies. Plus, they provide a swimming pool, a workout room, a lounge, washer, dryer, etc. Most have free toothpaste and razors, and all have free shampoo and soap.

3. They treat you like a customer, not a patient. $5 worth of tips a day will have the entire staff scrambling to help you. There is a city Bus stop out front, and seniors ride free. The Handicap bus will also pick you up (if you fake a decent limp). To meet other nice people, call a Church bus on Sundays. For a change of scenery, take the Airport shuttle Bus and eat at one of the nice restaurants there. While you're at the airport, fly somewhere. Otherwise, the cash keeps building up.

4. It takes months to get into decent nursing homes. Holiday Inn will take your reservation today. And you are not stuck in one place forever, you can move from Inn to Inn, or even from city to city. Want to see Hawaii? They have a Holiday Inn there too.

5. TV broken? Light bulbs need changing? Need a mattress replaced? No problem. They fix everything, and apologize for the inconvenience. The Inn has a night security person and daily room service. The maid checks to see if you are

ok. If not, they will call the undertaker or an ambulance. If you fall and break a hip, Medicare will pay for the hip, and Holiday Inn will upgrade you to a suite for the rest of your life.

6. And no worries about visits from family. They will always be glad to find you, and probably check in for a few days mini-vacation. The grand kids can use the pool. What more can you ask for?

So: As I reach the Golden age I'm facing it with a grin. I'll just check into the nearest Holiday Inn!

A man plays a game of poker with his friends every weekend. One evening he comes home after his game, and tells his wife to pack her bags, she is going to live with one of his poker buddies.

"What are you talking about?" she asks.

"I lost you to him in poker tonight, just pack your bags!"

"How could you lose me in a poker game," the exasperated woman asks.

"It wasn't easy; I had to fold with four aces."

Three elderly gentlemen were talking about what their grandchildren would be saying about them fifty years from now.

"I would like my grandchildren to say, 'He was successful in business'," declared the first man.

"Fifty years from now," said the second, "I want them to say, 'He was a loyal family man'."

Turning to the third gent, the first gent asked, "So what do you want them to say about you in fifty years?"

"Me?" the third man replied. "I want them all to say, "He certainly looks good for his age'!"

For the first time in many years, an old man traveled from his rural town to the city to attend a movie. After buying his ticket, he stopped at the concession stand to purchase some popcorn.

Handing the attendant $1.50, he couldn't help but comment, "The last time I came to the movies, popcorn was only 15 cents."

"Well, sir," the attendant replied with a grin, "You're really going to enjoy yourself. We have sound now."

Some thoughts from a retired mind

I was thinking about how a status symbol of today is those cell phones that everyone has clipped onto their belt or purse. I can't afford one, so, I'm wearing my garage door opener.

You know, I spent a fortune on deodorant before I realized that people who avoided me just didn't like me.

I was thinking that women should put pictures of missing husbands on beer cans, and men should put pictures of their missing wives up at the mall!

I was thinking about old age and decided that old age is when you still have something on the ball, but you are just too tired to bounce it.

I thought about making a fitness movie, for folks my age, and call it "Pumping Rust."

I have gotten that dreaded furniture disease: That's when your chest is falling into your drawers!

I've come to realize that the secret to a happy life is not looking like Barbie or Ken and suffering through tofu and rice cakes to stay that way! It's eating chocolate, staying chunky and explaining that you're really a perfect size 6, but you keep it covered with fat so it doesn't get scratched!

I know, when people see a cat's litter box, they always say, "Oh, have you got a cat?" Just once I want to say, "No, it's for Visitors!"

Employment application blanks always ask 'who is to be notified in case of an emergency' I think you should write, "A Good Doctor!"

Why is it that every time I lose weight it finds me again?

Why do they put pictures of criminals up in the Post Office? What are we supposed to do -- write to these men? Why don't they just put their pictures on the postage stamps so the mailmen could look for them while they deliver the mail? Or better yet, arrest them while they are taking their pictures!

Just once, when someone says, "How are you?" (without really wanting to know), I'd like to say "Well, I can't keep my teeth in, I pee on myself every time I laugh, my hair is falling out, I cannot see where the heck I'm going most of the time, my back hurts and I pass gas every time I sneeze (and feel like sneezing right now)! I'll bet that'd cure 'em from asking again!

The nice thing about being senile

is you can hide your own

Easter eggs.

A man and his bride are at a resort for their honeymoon. The resort offers horseback riding and they decide to give it a try. They start off down the trail, when a noise startles the bride's horse. It rears, jostling the bride. The groom jumps off his horse, grabs the reins of the horse, gets right into the horse's face, and says, "That's one!"

The couple rides a while longer. A flock of birds, startled by the horses, flies up out of the brush. Again, the bride's horse jumps back, and she bounces around in the saddle. The groom jumps off his horse, calms the bride's horse, look it in the eyes, and says, "That's two!"

Near the end of the ride, a rabbit runs in front of the couple. The bride's horse is spooked, and the bride falls from the saddle. The groom jumps off his horse, makes sure the bride is not injured, and then says to the horse, "That's three." He pulls out a gun and shoot the horse, killing it.

The appalled bride scream, "You are a sick man. You're a mean spirited and vicious human being! I can't believe that I married someone as heartless as you!"

The groom looks her in the eye and says, "That's one!"

THE NEW "OVER-40" BARBIES

1.) Bifocals Barbie. Comes with her own set of blended-lens fashion frames in six wild colors (half-frames too!), neck chain and large-print editions of Reader's Digest.

2.) Hot Flash Barbie. Press Barbie's bellybutton and watch her face turn beet red while tiny drops of perspiration appear on her forehead! With hand-held fan and tiny tissues.

3.) Facial Hair Barbie. As Barbie's hormone levels shift, see her whiskers grow! Available with teensy tweezers and magnifying mirror.

4.) Cook's Arms Barbie. Hide Barbie's droopy triceps with these new, roomier-sleeved gowns. Good news on the tummy front, too: muumuus are back! Cellulite cream and loofah sponge optional.

5.) Bunion Barbie. Years of disco dancing in stiletto heels have definitely taken their toll on Barbie's dainty arched feet. Soothe her sores with this pumice stone and plasters, then slip on soft terry mules. Colors: pink, rose, blush.

6.) No More Wrinkles Barbie. Erase those pesky crow's-feet and lip lines with a tube of Skin Sparkle-Spackle, from Barbie's own line of exclusive age-blasting cosmetics.

7.) Soccer Mom Barbie. All that experience as a cheerleader is really paying off as Barbie dusts off her old high school megaphone to root for Babs and Ken Jr. With minivan in robin's egg blue or white, and cooler filled with doughnut holes and fruit punch.

8.) Midlife Crisis Barbie. It's time to ditch Ken. Barbie needs a change, and Bruce (her personal trainer) is just what the doctor ordered, along with Prozac. They're hopping in her new red Miata and heading for the Napa Valley to open a B&B. Comes with real tape of "Breaking Up Is Hard to Do."

9.) Single Mother Barbie. There's not much time for primping anymore! Ken's shacked up with the Swedish au pair in the Dream House and Barbie's across town with Babs and Ken Jr. in a fourth-floor walk-up. Barbie's selling off her old gowns and accessories to raise rent money. Complete garage sale kit included.

10.) Recovery Barbie. Too many parties have finally caught up with the ultimate party girl. Now she does 12 steps instead of dance steps! Clean and sober, she's going to meetings religiously. Comes with little copy of The Big Book, and a six-pack of Diet Coke.

SENIORS TEXTING CODES

ATD - At The Doctors

BFF - Best Friend Fell

BTW - Bring the Wheelchair

BYOT - Bring Your Own Teeth

FWIW - Forgot Where I Was

GGPBL - Gotta Go Pacemaker Battery Low

IMHO - Is My Hearing-Aid On

LMDO - Laughing My Dentures Out

OMMR - On My Massage Recliner

ROFLACGU - Rolling On Floor Laughing And Can't Get Up...

What Generation Are You?

Welcome to the generational assessment test. Note your answer to each of the following questions and review your results at the end.

Who is the ideal figure of motherhood?
A - Eleanor Roosevelt
B - Donna Reed
C - Mrs. Brady
D - Lois Griffin

What did you want to be when you grew up?
A - Part of a nuclear family
B - Someone who makes lots of money
C - Living with your parents
D - Living with your parents

Music should be:
A - Melodic and romantic
B - Annoying to your parents
C - Annoying to your parents
D - Annoying to your parents

The scariest moment in film history was:
A - When the mummy rose from his tomb
B - When the Blob chased Steve McQueen
C - When the alien burst from the man's chest
D - Watching any of the Twilight movies

The most inspiring American is:
A - John Wayne
B - John F. Kennedy
C - John F. Kennedy Jr
D - The boys of South Park

I expect my retirement to be:

A - When I can look back on a happy, fulfilling life
B - An opportunity to finally write my novel
C - An agonizing slide into abject poverty
D - A daily struggle to survive in a horribly polluted world

America is becoming:
A - More impersonal
B - More frightening
C - More expensive
D - Whatever

The American Dream is:
A - A house with a two-car garage
B - A healthy family
C - Winning the lottery
D - Touring with Justin Bieber

My college major was:
A - Business
B - Liberal arts
C - Secondary to my bartending job
D - Something far, far away

A good meal would be:
A - Meat and potatoes
B - Vegetarian macrobiotic
C - From a drive-up window
D - Microwaveable

My favorite footwear is:
A - Sensible shoes
B - Earth shoes
C - Converse high-tops
D - Doc Martens

I learned to drive behind the wheel of a:
A - '53 Packard
B - '61 VW
C - '78 Pinto

D - PS3

The "woman":
A - Marilyn Monroe
B - Raquel Welch
C - Julia Roberts
D - Megan Fox

The "man":
A - Cary Grant
B - Paul McCartney
C - Eddie Vedder
D - Ryan Reynolds

Lost idol:
A - James Dean
B - Jim Morrison
C - Kurt Cobain
D - Mario Bros

Fashion accessory best forgotten:
A - Double knit
B - Bell bottoms
C - Skinny ties
D - Ridiculously baggy pants

The best way to spend a weekend is:
A - Playing golf
B - Consciousness raising
C - Mountain biking
D - Internet surfing

I remember where I was when:
A - The Japanese surrendered
B - John F. Kennedy was shot
C - John Lennon was shot
D - Brad and Angelina got engaged

Life changing movie:

A - East of Eden
B - Easy Rider
C - Heathers
D - Anchor Man

Life-changing novel:
A - Catcher in the Rye
B - Fear and Loathing in Las Vegas
C - Bright Lights Big City
D - Vampire Diaries

Sports hero:
A - Mickey Mantle
B - O.J. Simpson
C - Michael Jordan
D - Tebow

Celebrity my generation would rather not claim:
A - Joe McCarthy
B - Barry Manilow
C - Vanilla Ice
D - Hannah Montana

Computers are:
A - Frightening and disconcerting
B - Complicated
C - Part of life
D - My only link to the outside world

The father is the one who:
A - Brings home the bacon
B - Is attuned to his sensitive side
C - Left years ago
D - Holds the remote control

My after-college plans:
A - Work hard to help build a strong America
B - Take my pick of many job opportunities
C - Take my pick of many low-paying temp services

D - Would you like fries with that?

My generation's most annoying fad is:
A - Nuclear testing
B - Hula hoops
C - Body piercing
D - Unemployment

The voice of my generation:
A - Walter Cronkite
B - Bob Dylan
C - Madonna
D - Kim Kardashian

My generation's biggest fear is:
A - Heart disease
B - Getting older
C - Collection agencies
D - Not getting likes on Facebook

RESULTS:

If you answer mostly A, you're a pre-boomer. If you answer mostly B, you're a Baby-Boomer. If you answer mostly C, you're in Generation X. If you answer mostly D, you're in Generation Y.

Aging Is When...

1. *Everything hurts and what doesn't hurt, doesn't work.*

2. *The gleam in your eye is the sun hitting your bifocals.*

3. *You feel like the night after, but you haven't been anywhere.*

4. *Your little black book contains only names ending in M.D.*

5. *You get winded playing chess.*

6. *Your children begin to look middle-aged.*

7. *You finally reach the top of the ladder and find it leaning.*

8. *You join a health club, but don't go.*

9. *You begin to outlive enthusiasm.*

10. *Your mind makes contracts that your body can't keep.*

11. *You look forward to a dull evening.*

12. *"25 Years Ago Today", is your favorite part of the newspaper.*

13. *You sit in a rocking chair and can't get it going.*

14. *Your knees buckle and your belt won't.*

15. *The best part of the day is over when the alarm clock goes off.*

16. *Your back goes out more often than you do.*

17. You sink your teeth into a steak and they stay there.

18. You forget, why you are reading this.

A man is enjoying a late night drink when he notices that a man who must have had too much to drink has fallen from his stool. He runs over and puts him back on the stool, only to watch him fall again a few minutes later.

He feels sorry for the man and calls a cab after getting the man's address from his driver's license. The man has a terrible time making it to the cab, falling down three more times. The Good Samaritan decides it would be best to ride with the man to insure his safe arrival home.

The man stumbles and falls two more times from the cab to the front door.

Hearing a commotion, the man's wife opens the front door.

"Ma'am, I brought your husband home," the Samaritan exclaims.

"Thank you so much, but where's his wheelchair?" asks the wife.

Driving through a small town, a man comes to an intersection where the cross traffic has the right of way. Instead of coming to a full stop, he slows, notices a break in traffic and makes a right turn. No sooner had he turned than a cop puts on his lights and pulls the man over.

"You didn't stop at that intersection," says the cop.

"I know officer, but I did slow down," replies the man.

"Yes, but you didn't stop."

"No, but I slowed down."

"But you didn't stop," the cop angrily replies.

"No, but what is the difference really?" asks the young man.

The cop takes out his nightstick and starts to hit the young man. "Now, what do you want me to do," he asks, "slow down or stop?"

Submitted from a fan:

Today at the drugstore, the clerk was a gent.
From my purchase this chap took off ten percent.
I asked for the cause of a lesser amount;
And he answered, "Because of the Seniors Discount."

I went to McDonald's for a burger and fries;
And there, once again, got quite a surprise.
The clerk poured some coffee, which he handed to me.
He said, "For you, Seniors, the coffee is free."

Understand---I'm not old---I'm merely mature;
But some things are changing, temporarily, I'm sure.
The newspaper print gets smaller each day,
And people speak softer---can't hear what they say.

My teeth are my own (I have the receipt.),
and my glasses identify people I meet.
Oh, I've slowed down a bit... not a lot, I am sure.
You see, I'm not old... I'm only mature.

The gold in my hair has been bleached by the sun.
You should see all the damage that chlorine has done.
Washing my hair has turned it all white,
But don't call it gray... saying "blond" is just right.

My car is all paid for... not a nickel is owed.

Yet a kid yells, "Old duffer... get off of the road!"
My car has no scratches... not even a dent.
Still I get all that guff from a punk who's "Hell bent."

My friends all get older... much faster than me.
They seem much more wrinkled, from what I can see.
I've got "character lines," not wrinkles... for sure,
But don't call me old... just call me mature.

The steps in the houses they're building today
Are so high that they take... your breath all away;
And the streets are much steeper than ten years ago.
That should explain why my walking is slow.

But I'm keeping up on what's hip and what's new,
And I think I can still dance a mean boogaloo.
I'm still in the running... in this I'm secure,
I'm not really old... I'm only mature.

Silly Jokes & Amazing Tricks

Christopher & Olivia James

Branson, Missouri, USA

Where do ants go for their holidays?
Frants!

What do you call an ant who skips school?
A truant!

What do you get if you cross some ants with some tics?
All sorts of antics!

What medicine would you give an ill ant?
Antibiotics!

What games to ants play with elephants?
Squash!

What do you call a 100 year old ant?
An antique!

What is the biggest ant in the world?
An elephant!

Why don't anteaters get sick?
Because they are full of antibodies!

What do you call an ant who likes to be alone?
An independant!

What kind of ant is good at maths?
An accountant!

What animal do you look like when you get into the bath?
A little bear!

Why do bees hum?
Because they've forgotten the words!

What kind of bees hum and drop things?
A fumble bee!

What do bees do if they want to use public transport?
Wait at a buzz stop!

What do bees chew?
Bumble gum!

What did the bee to the other bee in summer?
Swarm here isn't it!

What is a bee's favorite classical music composer?
Bee-thoven!

Where do bees go on holiday?
Stingapore!

What do you call a bee who's had a spell put on him?
He's bee-witched!

Why do bees buzz?
Because they can't whistle!

Can bees fly in the rain?
Not without their little yellow jackets!

What goes zzub, zzub?
A bee flying backwards!

What are the smartest bees?
Spelling bees!

What bee is good for your health?
Vitamin bee!

Why did the queen bee kick out all of the other bees?
Because they kept droning on and on!

What do you call a bee born in May?
A maybe!

What kind of bee can't be understood?

A mumble bee!

What did the bee say to the naughty bee?
Bee-hive yourself!

Why do bees have sticky hair?
Because of the honey combs!

What do cats eat for breakfast?
Mice Crispies.

Why do cats like to hear other cats make noise?
It's meow-sic to their ears!

Why does everyone love cats?
They're purr-fect!

What do you call a cat who eats lemons?
A sourpuss!

What do you call it when a cat bites?
Catnip!

What's every cat's favorite song?
Three Blind Mice!

What do you call it when a cat stops?

A paws!

What kind of cats lay around the house?

Car-pets!

How do cats buy things?

From a cat-alogue!

What time is it when an elephant sits on the fence?

Time to fix the fence!

What's gray, carries a bunch of flowers and cheers you up when your ill?

A get wellephant!

Policeman: "One of your elephants has been seen chasing a man on a bicycle."

Zoo Keeper: "Nonsense, none of my elephants knows how to ride a bicycle!"

Why do the elephants have short tails?

Because they can't remember long stories!

What's the difference between an African elephant and an Indian elephant?

About 3,000 miles!

Teacher: "Name six wild animals"

Pupil: " Four elephants and two lions!"

What's as big as an elephant but weighs nothing?

An elephant's shadow!

How do you know when there is an elephant under your bed?

When your nose touches the ceiling!

Why were the elephants thrown out of the swimming pool?

Because they couldn't hold their trunks up.

John: I lost my pet dinosaur.

Ron: Why don't you put an ad in the newspaper?

John: What good would that do, she can't read!

What did the Tyrannosaurus rex get after mopping the floor?

Dino-sore!

What do you call a dinosaur that never gives up?

Try-Try-Try-ceratops!

What do you call a dinosaur that smashes everything in its path?

Tyrannosaurus wrecks!

Which dinosaur slept all day?
The dino-snore!

What do you call Tyrannosaurus rex when it wears a cowboy hat and boots?
Tyrannosaurus tex!

What kind of dinosaur can you ride in a rodeo?
A Bronco-saurus!

What's an astronauts favorite drink?

Gravi-tea.

How do you make a baby sleep on a space ship?
You rocket.

What do space cows say?
"Mooooo-n."

What do you call a pan spinning through space?
An unidentified frying object.

What do you call a wizard in space?
A flying saucer-er.

What did the left hand say to the right hand?
How does it feel to always be right?

What did one eye say to the other?
Between me and you, something smells.

Why don't acrobats work in the winter?
They only do Summer-saults.

What do you comb a rabbit with?
A hare brush.

Which rodent won the basketball game?

The porcupine because he had the most points.

What's the difference between a guitar and a fish?

You can't tuna fish.

How do you buy cat food?

Purrr can.

What monkey is always exploding?

A ba-boom.

Why can't you play games in the jungle?

Because there's always gonna be a cheetah.

Three sons left home, went out on their own and prospered.

They discussed the gifts they were able to give their elderly mother.

The first said: "I built a big house for our mother."

The second said: "I sent her a Mercedes with a driver."

The third said: "You remember how our mother enjoys reading the Bible. Now she can't see very well. So I sent her a remarkable parrot that recites the entire Bible. It took elders in the church 12 years to teach him. Mama just has to name the chapter and verse and the parrot recites it."

Soon thereafter, their mother sent out her letters of thanks.

"Milton," she said, "the house you built is so huge. I live only in one room, but I have to clean the whole house.

"Gerald," she said, "I am too old to travel. I stay most of the time at home so I rarely use the Mercedes. And that driver is so rude! He's a pain!"

"But Donald," she said, "the little chicken you sent was delicious!"

Why was the doctor mad?
Because he had no patients!

What is the best time to go to the dentist?
2:30 (tooth hurty)!

What is a polygon?
A dead parrot!

What do you get if you cross a duck with a firework?
A firequaker!

What is a parrot's favorite game?
Hide and Speak!

Why did the parrot wear a raincoat?
Because she wanted to be a Polly unsaturated!

What did the gamekeeper say to the lord of the manor?
'The pheasants are revolting'!

What is the definition of Robin?
A bird who steals!

What do you give a sick bird?
Tweetment!

What's another name for a clever duck?
A wise quacker!

What do you call a crate of ducks?
A box of quackers!

How do you know that owls are cleverer than chickens?
Have you ever heard of Kentucky-fried owl!

How do you get a parrot to talk properly?
Send him to polytechnic!

Where do birds invest their money?
In the stork market!

What do you get if you cross a parrot with a woodpecker?
A bird that talks in morse code!

What birds spend all their time on their knees?

Birds of prey!

What did they call the canary that flew into the pastry dish?

Tweetie Pie!

What kind of birds do you usually find locked up?

Jail-birds!

Why is a sofa like a roast chicken?

Because they're both full of stuffing!

What happens when ducks fly upside down?

They quack up!

What do you get if you cross a woodpecker with a carrier pigeon?

A bird who knocks before delivering its message!

What happened when the owl lost his voice?

He didn't give a hoot!

What do you get if you cross a cat with a bottle of vinegar?

A sourpuss!

What do you get if you cross a cat with a canary?

A peeping tom!

How does a lion greet the other animals in the field?
'Pleased to eat you.'!

What do you get if you cross a tiger with a snowman?
Frostbite!

What is a French cat's favorite pudding?
Chocolate mousse!

What happened when the lion ate the comedian?
He felt funny!

How is cat food sold?
Usually purr can!

What does the lion say to his friends before they go out hunting for food?
'Let us prey.'

What's the unluckiest kind of cat to have?
A catastrophe!

What do you get if you cross a cat with a tree?
A cat-a-logue!

Why was the cat so small?

Because it only ate condensed milk!

What do cows read in the morning?

Moospapers!

Why did the cat frown when she passed the hen house?

Because she heard fowl language!

How is a cat laying down like a coin?

Because he has his head on one side and his tail on the other!

Why did the cat sleep under the car?

Because she wanted to wake up oily!

What did the cat do when he swallowed some cheese?

He waited by the mouse hole with baited breath!

What do you call a lioin who has eaten your mother's sister?

An aunt-eater!

Why did the cat put the letter "M" into the fridge?

Because it turns "ice" into "mice"!

What does a lion brush his mane with?

A catacomb!

What do you get if cross a cat with a canary?

Shredded tweet!

What does a caterpillar do on New Years Day?

Turns over a new leaf!

What pillar doesn't need holding up?

A caterpillar!

Why was the centipede late?

Because he was playing "This little Piggy" with his baby brother!

What do you get if you cross a centipede and a parrot?

A walkie talkie!

What do you get if you cross a centipede and a chicken?

Enough drumsticks to feed an army!

What goes 99-clonk, 99-clonk, 99-clonk?

A centipede with a wooden leg!

Why did the turtle cross the road?

To get to the shell station

Why did the cow cross the road?

To get to the udder side!

Why did the chicken end up in the soup?

Because it ran out of cluck!

What do chickens grow on?

Eggplants!

Why did the chicken cross the basketball court?

He heard the referee calling fowls

Why is it easy for chicks to talk?
Because talk is cheep!

What do you call a rooster who wakes you up at the same time every morning?
An alarm cluck!

What do chicken families do on Saturday afternoon?
They go on peck-nics!

How long do chickens work?
Around the cluck!

Why did the chick disappoint his mother?
He wasn't what he was cracked up to be!

Is chicken soup good for your health?
Not if you're the chicken!

Why did the chicken cross the road, roll in the mud and cross the road again?
Because he was a dirty double-crosser!

Why didn't the chicken skeleton cross the road?

Because he didn't have enough guts!

Why did the chicken cross the playground?
To get to the other slide!

Why did the man put his money in the freezer?
He wanted cold hard cash!

What do you get when you cross a snowman with a vampire?
Frostbite.

How do crazy people go through the forest?
They take the psycho path.

What do prisoners use to call each other?
Cell phones.

What do you get from a pampered cow?
Spoiled milk.

Where do polar bears vote?
The North Poll

Where do snowmen keep their money?
In snow banks.

Why do sea-gulls fly over the sea?

Because if they flew over the bay they would be bagels!

What dog keeps the best time?

A watch dog.

Why did the tomato turn red?

It saw the salad dressing!

What did the grape do when it got stepped on?

It let out a little wine!

How do you make a tissue dance?

Put a little boogey in it!

Where do bees go to the bathroom?

At the BP station!

What did the judge say when the skunk walked in the court room?

Odor in the court.

What did the water say to the boat?
Nothing, it just waved.

Why don't skeletons fight each other?
They don't have the guts.

Knock Knock Jokes
Knock Knock!
Who's there?
Cargo!

Cargo who?

CarGo Beep Beep!

Knock Knock!

Who's there?

Cows.

Cows who?

Cows go moo, not who!

Knock Knock!

Who's there?

Boo.

Boo who?

Don't cry, it's only a joke!

Knock Knock!

Who's there?

Rita.

Rita who?

Rita book, you might learn something!

Knock Knock!

Who's there?

Heaven.

Heaven who?

Heaven you heard enough of these silly Knock Knock jokes?

Knock Knock!

Who's there?

Lettuce.

Lettuce who?

Lettuce in, its cold outside!

Knock Knock!

Who's there?

Anita.

Anita who?

Anita tissue....ah-choo! Too late!

Knock Knock!

Who's there?

Honeycomb.

Honeycomb who?

Honeycomb your hair!

Knock Knock!

Who's there?

Justin.

Justin who?

Justin time for dinner!

Knock Knock!

Who's there?

Canoe.

Canoe who?

Canoe come out to play?

Knock Knock!

Who's there?

Beets.

Beets who?

Beets me!

Knock Knock!

Who's there?

Duey.

Duey who?

Duey have to keep telling Knock Knock jokes.

Why do dogs bury bones in the ground?

Because you can't bury them in trees!

Why did the poor dog chase his own tail?

He was trying to make both ends meet!

What do you get if you cross a sheepdog with a rose?

A collie-flower!

Why do dogs wag their tails?
"Because no one else will do it for them!"

Why didn't the dog speak to his foot?
Because it's not polite to talk back to your paw!

What is the dogs favorite city?
New Yorkie!

What did the cowboy say when the bear ate Lassie?
"Well, doggone!"

How can if you have a stupid dog?
It chases parked cars!

What time is it when an elephant sits on the fence?
Time to fix the fence!

What' s grey with red spots?
An elephant with the measles!

What's big and grey and wears a mask?
The elephantom of the opera!

What do you call an elephant at the North Pole?
Lost!

Why were the elephants thrown out of the swimming pool?
Because they couldn't hold their trunks up!

What do you call an arctic cow?
An eskimoo!

Why does a rooster watch TV?
For hentertainment!

What do you call a crate of ducks?
A box of quackers!

Which fish can perform operations?
A Sturgeon!

What do you call a fish with no eyes?
Fsh!

What lives in the ocean, is grouchy and hates neighbors?
A hermit crab!

What do you get from a bad-tempered shark?
As far away as possible!

Why did the whale cross the road?

To get to the other tide!

What insect runs away from everything?
A flee!

What is the difference between a flea and a wolf?
One prowls on the hairy and the other howls on the prairie!

What to you call a Russian flea?
A Moscow-ito!

What do you get if you cross a rabbit and a flea?
Bugs Bunny!

How do you find where a flea has bitten you?
Start from scratch!

How do fireflies start a race?
Ready steady glow!

What is the difference between a fly and a bird?
A bird can fly but a fly can't bird!

Why is it better to be a grasshopper than a cricket?
Because grasshoppers can play cricket but crickets can't play grasshopper!

What is green and can jump a mile in a minute?
A grasshopper with hiccups!

Where would you put an injured insect?
In an antbulance!

How do you know if you have a tough mosquito?
You slap him and he slaps you back!

What do you get if you cross the Batman with an insect?
The Masked-quito!

What has antlers and sucks blood?
A moose-quito!

What is a mosquito's favorite sport?
Skin-diving!

Why are mosquitos religious?
They prey on you!

What do insects learn at school?
Mothmatics!

What's the biggest moth in the world?
A mammoth!

What's pretty, delicate and carries a sub machine gun?
A killer butterfly!

Why was the moth so unpopular?
He kept picking holes in everything!

What did Tom get when he locked Jerry in the freezer?
Mice cubes!

What mouse was a Roman emperor?
Julius Cheeser!

What do you get if you cross a frog and a dog?
A croaker spaniel!

What does a spider do when he gets angry?
He goes up the wall!

Why are spiders good swimmers?
They have webbed feet!

How do you spot a modern spider?
He doesn't have a web he had a website!

What did the spider say to the fly?
We're getting married do you want to come to the webbing?

Why was the glow worm unhappy?
Because her children weren't that bright!

What reads and lives in an apple?
A bookworm!

What did the woodworm say to the chair?
It's been nice gnawing you!

Why are glow worms good to carry in your bag?

They can lighten your load!

What do you get if you cross a dog with a airplane?
A jet setter!

Where do Eskimos train their dogs?
In the mush room!

Why did the snowman call his dog Frost?
Because frost bites!

Why don't dogs make good dancers?
Because they have two left feet!

What kind of dog does Dracula have?
A bloodhound!

What is the only kind of dog you can eat?
A hot dog!

What's yellow on the outside and grey on the inside?
An elephant disguised as a banana!

What's grey, carries a bunch of flowers and cheers you up when your ill?
A get wellephant!

What' s grey, has four legs and jumps up and down?
An elephant on a trampoline!

What's grey and wrinkly and jumps every twenty seconds?
An elephant with hiccups!

What's as big as an elephant but weighs nothing?
An elephant's shadow!

How do you know when there is an elephant under your bed?
When your nose touches the ceiling!

What did the grape say when the elephant stood on it?
Nothing, it just let out a little wine!

What kind of doctor treats ducks?
A quack!

What did the well mannered sheep say to his friend at the field gate?
After ewe!

Why did the ram fall over the cliff?
He didn't see the ewe turn!

Blooie Balloons

A RED BALLOON IS SHOWN. IN A FLASH, A LOUD REPORT IS HEARD, AND THE RED BALLOON CHANGES TO YELLOW!

PREPARE THIS TRICK BY STUFFING A YELLOW BALLOON INSIDE A RED ONE. BLOW UP THE INNER YELLOW BALLOON, THE RED ONE WILL SWELL UP WITH IT. TIE THE NECK OF THE YELLOW BALLOON WITH A RUBBER BAND. NOW BLOW MORE AIR INTO THE RED ONE TO CAUSE AN AIR POCKET BETWEEN THE BALLOONS. HOLDING THE RED BALLOON ALOFT, PRICK IT WITH A SECRETLY HELD PIN. THE RED ONE WILL BURST AND THE YELLOW BALLOON REMAINS!

What do cows like to dance to?
Any kind of moosic you like!

Where do sheep get shaved?
At the baa baas!

What do you give a pony with a cold?
Cough Stirrup!

What is a horse's favorite sport?
Stable tennis!

What did the farmer call the cow that would not give him any milk?

An udder failure!

What do you give a sick pig?

Oinkment!

What is a pigs favorite ballet?

Swine Lake!

What do you get if you cross a hen with a dog?

Pooched eggs!

Why did the pony cough?

Because he was a little horse!

What is the opposite of cock-a doodle-doo?

Cock-a-doodle-don't!

Where do milkshakes come from?

Excited cows!

Where do shellfish go to borrow money?

To the prawn broker!

What happened to the shark who swallowed a bunch of keys?

He got lockjaw!

Where do fish wash?

In a river basin!

What fish only swims at night?

A starfish!

Which fish go to heaven when they die?

Angelfish!

What is the best way to communicate with a fish?

Drop it a line!

What kind of horse can swim underwater without coming up for air?

A seahorse!

Where do frogs keep their money?

In a river bank!

What kind of bull doesn't have horns?

A bullfrog!

What jumps up and down in front of a car?
Froglights!

Why was the frog down in the mouth?
He was un hoppy!

Whats green and can jump a mile a minute?
A frog with hiccups!

Why did the lizard go on a diet?
It weighed too much for its scales!

What do toads drink?
Croaka-cola!

What do you get if cross a science fiction film with a toad?
Star Warts!

What kind of shoes to frogs like?
Open toad sandals!

What goes up and down but does not move?
Stairs

Where should a 500 pound alien go?
On a diet

What did one toilet say to the other?
You look a bit flushed.

Why did the picture go to jail?
Because it was framed.

What did one wall say to the other wall?
I'll meet you at the corner.

What did the paper say to the pencil?
Write on!

What do you call a boy named Lee that no one talks to?
Lonely

What gets wetter the more it dries?
A towel.

Why do bicycles fall over?
Because they are two-tired!

Why do dragons sleep during the day?
So they can fight knights!

What did Cinderella say when her photos did not show up?
Someday my prints will come!

Why was the broom late?
It over swept!

What part of the car is the laziest?
The wheels, because they are always tired!

What did the stamp say to the envelope?
Stick with me and we will go places!

We're you long in the hospital?

No, I was the same size I am now!

Why couldn't the pirate play cards?
Because he was sitting on the deck!

What did one elevator say to the other elevator?
I think I'm coming down with something!

Why was the belt arrested?
Because it held up some pants!

Why was everyone so tired on April 1st?
They had just finished a March of 31 days.

Why can't your nose be 12 inches long?
Because then it would be a foot!

What makes the calendar seem so popular?
Because it has a lot of dates!

What is it that even the most careful person overlooks?
Her nose!

Did you hear about the robbery last night?
Two clothes pins held up a pair of pants!

Why do you go to bed every night?
Because the bed won't come to you!

Why did Billy go out with a prune?
Because he couldn't find a date!

Why do eskimos do their laundry in Tide?
Because it's too cold out-tide!

What has four wheels and flies?
A garbage truck!

What kind of car does Mickey Mouse's wife drive?
A minnie van!

Why don't traffic lights ever go swimming?
Because they take too long to change!

Why did the man run around his bed?
To catch up on his sleep!

Why did the robber take a bath before he stole from the bank?
He wanted to make a clean get away!

Why did the policeman go to the baseball game?

She heard someone had stolen a base!

Why did the book join the police?
He wanted to go undercover!

Why was there thunder and lightning in the lab?
The scientists were brainstorming!

What do lawyers wear to court?
Lawsuits!

What did the lawyer name his daughter?
Sue

What kind of card does a farmer drive?
A cornvertable!

What do you call a flying police officer?
A helicopper!

How did the farmer mend his pants?
With cabbage patches!

Why did the lazy man want a job in a bakery?
So he could loaf around!

Why did the farmer ride his horse to town?

It was too heavy to carry!

What do you call a happy cowboy?

A jolly rancher.

When does a doctor get mad?

When he runs out of patients!

Why did the pillow go to the doctor?

He was feeling all stuffed up!

Bloody Puzzler

ASK SOMEONE TO HOLD A RULER
IN ONE HAND, AND A PENCIL IN THE
OTHER. AS YOUR BACK IS TURNED,
REQUEST THAT HE HOLD JUST ONE
OF THE OBJECTS HIGH OVER HIS
HEAD. AFTER A FEW MINUTES,
TELL HIM TO PLACE BOTH OBJECTS
ON THE TABLE, STILL HOLDING THEM.
TURNING AROUND, YOU NOW TELL
HIM WHICH OBJECT HE HELD ALOFT!
THE SECRET IS IN THE PERSON'S
HANDS. THE HAND THAT WAS RAISED
WILL BE PALER THAN THE OTHER
AND THE VEINS SMALLER DUE TO
THE BLOOD LEAVING IT AS IT WAS
RAISED!

What did on tonsil say to the other tonsil?

Get dressed up, the doctor is taking us out!

Did you hear the one about the germ?

Never mind, I don't want to spread it around

Where does a boat go when it's sick?

To the dock!

Why did the cookie go to the hospital?

He was feeling really crumbie!

What did the judge say to the dentist?

Do you swear to pull the tooth, the whole tooth and nothing but the tooth?

Why did the tree go to the dentist?

To get a root canal.

Why did the king go to the dentist?

To get his teeth crowned!

What time do you go to the dentist?

Tooth-Hurty!

What does a dentist do during an earthquake?

She braces herself!

What did the tooth say to the dentist as she was leaving?
Fill me in when you get back

What is a dentist's favorite animal?
A molar bear!

What did the dentist get for an award?
A little plaque

What has one head, one foot and four legs?
A Bed

Did you hear the joke about the roof?
Never mind, it's over your head!

How many letters are in The Alphabet?
There are 11 letters in The Alphabet

How can you spell cold with two letters?
IC (icy)

If you were in a race and passed the person in 2nd place,
what place would you be in?
2nd place!

What is the center of gravity?
The letter V!

What has a head, a tail, is brown, and has no legs?
A penny!

What goes up, but never comes down?
Your age!

What gets bigger and bigger as you take more away from it?
A hole!

How many months have 28 days?
All of them!

How many books can you put into an empty backpack?
One! After that it's not empty.

Which weighs more, a ton of feathers or a ton of bricks?
Neither, they both weigh a ton!

Does your shirt have holes in it?
No, then how did you put it on?

What starts with a P and ends with an E and has a million letters in it?

Post Office!

When does a cart come before a horse?

In the dictionary!

What is full of holes but can still hold water?

A sponge!

What has two hands, a round face, always runs, but stays in place?

A clock!

Where does success come before work?

In the dictionary!

What breaks when you say it?

Silence!

What did the ground say to the earthquake?

You crack me up!

Why did the music teacher need a ladder?

To reach the high notes.

Why did nose not want to go to school?
He was tired of getting picked on!

How do you get straight A's?
By using a ruler!

Why did the kid study in the airplane?
Because he wanted a higher education!

How did the music teacher get locked in the classroom?
His keys were inside the piano!

What do elves learn in school?
The elf-abet!

What object is king of the classroom?
The ruler!

How does the barber cut the moon's hair?
E-clipse it!

What happened when the wheel was invented?
It caused a revolution!

What do librarians take with them when they go fishing?
Bookworms

What is the world's tallest building?

The library because it has the most stories.

What vegetables to librarians like?

Quiet peas.

Why did the clock in the cafeteria run slow?

It always went back four seconds.

Why didn't the sun go to college?

Because it already had a million degrees!

Why were the early days of history called the dark ages?
Because there were so many knights!

Why is England the wettest country?
Because the queen has reigned there for years!

How did the Vikings send secret messages?
By norse code!

What kind of lighting did Noah use for the ark?
Floodlights!

What did Mason say to Dixon?
We've got to draw the line here!

Who made King Arthur's round table?
Sir-Cumference

Who built the ark?
I have Noah idea!

Where was the Declaration of Independence signed?
At the bottom!

What is the fruitiest subject at school?

History, because it's full of dates!

When a knight was killed in battle, what sign did they put on his grave?

Rust in peace!

How was the Roman Empire cut in half?

With a pair of Caesars!

Why didn't the quarter roll down the hill with the nickel?

Because it had more cents.

Why was the math book sad?

Because it had too many problems.

What kind of meals do math teachers eat?

Square meals!

Why didn't the two 4's want any dinner?

Because they already 8!

What is a math teacher's favorite sum?

Summer!

What do you get when you divide the circumference of a Jack-o-lantern by its diameter?

Pumpkin Pi!

What did zero say to the number eight?
Nice belt.

Why did the teacher wear sunglasses?
Because his class was so bright!

Why were the teacher's eyes crossed?
She couldn't control her pupils!

Teacher: You missed school yesterday, didn't you?
Student: Not really.

Teacher: If I had 6 oranges in one hand and 7 apples in the other, what would I have?
Student: Big hands!

Teacher: If you got $20 from 5 people, what you get?
Student: A new bike.

Teacher: I hope I didn't see you looking at John's exam?
Student: I hope you didn't either.

Teacher: What is the shortest month?
Student: May, it only has three letters.

Why did the teacher turn the lights on?
Because her class was so dim.

Where do the pianists go for vacation?
Florida Keys

What is the smartest state?
Alabama, it has four A's and one B.

Where to pencils come from?
Pennsylvania!

Teacher: Where is the English Channel?
Student: I don't know, my TV doesn't pick it up!

What is the capital of Alaska?
Come on, Juneau this one!

What rock group has four men that don't sing?
Mount Rushmore!

What city cheats at exams?
Peking!

What is the capital of Washington?

The W!

What did Delaware?

Her New Jersey!

Multiplying Coins

YOU PLACE 4 COINS ON THE TABLE. YOU NOW TELL YOUR FRIENDS THAT YOU CAN, WITH YOUR MYSTERIOUS POWERS, CAUSE THE 4 COINS TO CONVERT INTO 5! SECRETLY, YOU HAVE ATTACHED A COIN (WITH A DAB OF SOAP) TO THE UNDERSIDE OF THE TABLE. BRUSH THE COINS INTO YOUR CUPPED LEFT HAND AND AT THE SAME TIME RELEASE THE HIDDEN COIN. IMMEDIATELY MAKE A FIST AROUND THE COINS. ASK SOMEONE TO TOUCH YOUR FIST, THEN OPEN YOUR HAND, AND BEHOLD.... THERE ARE FIVE COINS!

What is the fastest country in the world?
Rush-a!

Teacher: What can you tell me about the Dead Sea?
Student: I didn't even know it was sick!

How can you tell the ocean is friendly?

It waves.

What kind of hair do oceans have?
Wavy!

What did Mars say to Saturn?
Give me a ring sometime.

What did the big flower say to the small flower?
What's up Bud.

Where does seaweed go to look for a job?
The kelp wanted section.

When is the moon the heaviest?
When it's full!

What type of songs do the planets sing?
Nep-tunes!

What kind of flower grows on your face?
Tulips!

What washes up on very small beaches?
Microwaves!

What do you call an attractive volcano?
Lava-ble!

What did the tornado say to the sports car?
Want to go for a spin!

What kind of shorts to clouds wear?
Thunderwear!

What's a tornado's favorite game?
Twister!

What did one volcano say to the other volcano?
I lava you!

What bow can't be tied?
A rainbow!

What falls but never hits the ground?
The temperature!

What happens when the fog disperses in California?
UCLA!

What did the tree wear to the pool party?
Swimming trunks!

What did the beaver say to the tree?
It's been nice gnawing you!

What is a tree's least favorite month?
Sep-timber!

What kind of tree can fit into your hand?
A palm tree!

How do trees get on the internet?
They log in.

How can you tell that a tree is a dogwood tree?
By its bark!

What did the little tree say to the big tree?
Leaf me alone!

Why did the pine tree get into trouble?
Because it was being knotty

What did the tree do when the bank closed?
It started a new branch

What do you call cheese that isn't yours?

Nacho cheese!

Why do the French like to eat snails?
Because they don't like fast food!

Why did the fisherman put peanut butter into the sea?
To go with the jellyfish!

Why shouldn't you tell an egg a joke?
Because it might crack up!

What did the baby corn say to it's mom?
Where is pop corn?

What kind of nuts always seems to have a cold?
Cashews!

Waiter, will my pizza be long?
No sir, it will be round!

What is green and sings?
Elvis Parsley

Why did the banana go to the doctor?
Because it wasn't peeling well!

What candy do you eat on the playground?

Recess pieces.

Why don't you starve in a desert?

Because of all the 'sand which is' there.

How do you make a walnut laugh?

Crack it up!

In which school do you learn to make ice cream?

Sunday School.

What do elves make sandwiches with?
Shortbread

Why shouldn't you tell a secret on a farm?
Because the potatoes have eyes and the corn has ears.

What is a pretzel's favorite dance?
The Twist!

What are twins favorite fruit?
Pears!

If a crocodile makes shoes, what does a banana make?
Slippers!

What do you give to a sick lemon?
Lemon aid!

Why did the lady love to drink hot chocolate?
Because she was a cocoanut!

How do you make a milk shake?
Give it a good scare!

What do you call a peanut in a spacesuit?
An astronut!

What kind of keys to kids like to carry?
Cookies!

Why don't they serve chocolate in prison?
Because it makes you break out!

What is a cow's favorite day?
Moo-years Day!

What do you get when you plant kisses?
Two lips.

Where does the Easter bunny get his breakfast?
IHOP!

How does the Easter bunny stay in shape?
Lots of eggercise!

What was the most popular dance in 1776?
Indepen-dance!

What do you call a fake stone in Ireland?
A sham rock

Why does Santa Claus like to go down the chimney?

Because it soots him!

What do Santa's elves do after school?
Their gnomework!

What do snowmen like to eat for breakfast?
Frosted Flakes!

What is a parent's favorite Christmas carol?
Silent Night.

What is the fear of Santa Claus called?
Claustrophobia

What nationality is Santa Claus?
North Polish!

Why does Santa have a garden?
So he can hoe, hoe, hoe!

Why did the dog hand up his stocking at Christmas?
He was waiting for Santa Paws.

Why is it cold on Christmas?
Because it's in Decembrrrrrrrrr!

What happened when the turkey got into a fight?
He got the stuffing knocked out of him!

Who isn't hungry on Thanksgiving?
The turkey, because he's already stuffed!

Who was the drummer in the Thanksgiving band?
The turkey, because he had the drumsticks!

What do you call a single vampire?
A bat-chelor.

Why didn't the skeleton cross the road?
He didn't have the guts!

Why are graveyards noisy?
Because of all the coffin!

What is a scarecrows favorite fruit?
Straw-berries!

What did the boy ghost say to the girl ghost?
You sure are Boo-tiful!

Why was the baby ghost sad?
He wanted his mummy!

What do witches put on their bagels?

Scream Cheese

What did the vampire say about the Dracula movie?

It was fang-tastic!

Why are vampires tough to get along with?

Because they can be pains in the neck!

Do you know how to make a witch itch?

You take away the w!

What subject in school is easy for a witch?

Spell-ing

What do you call a cow that won't give milk?

A milk dud!

When is a well dressed lion like a weed?

When he's a dandelion (dandy lion)

What do you call a sleeping bull?

A bull-dozer.

Why do gorillas have big nostrils?

Because they have big fingers!

Why are teddy bears never hungry?

They are always stuffed!

Why are fish so smart?

Because they live in schools.

What happened when the lion ate the comedian?
He felt funny!

What fish only swims at night?
A starfish!

Why is a fish easy to weigh?
Because it has its own scales!

Why did the lion spit out the clown?
Because he tasted funny!

What do you get when you cross a snake and a pie?
A pie-thon!

What did the buffalo say to his son when he went away on a trip?
Bison!

Why didn't the boy believe the tiger?
He thought it was a lion!

How do bees get to school?
By school buzz!

What do you call a bear with no ears?
B!

What animal has more lives than a cat?
Frogs, they croak every night!

What do you call a dinosaur with no eyes?
Doyouthinkysaraus

What do you call a sleeping dinosaur?
A dino-snore!

What dinosaur would Harry Potter be?
The Dinosorcerer

Why was the Stegosaurus such a good volleyball player?
Because he could really spike the ball!

What does a triceratops sit on?
Its tricera-bottom.

What do dinosaurs use on the floors of their kitchens?
Rep-tiles

What's the nickname for someone who put their right hand in the mouth of a T-Rex?

Lefty

What do you call a paleontologist who sleeps all the time?
Lazy bones

What do you get when a dinosaur scores a touchdown?
A dino-score

What did the dinosaur use to build his house?
A dino-saw

What do you call four bullfighters in quicksand?
Quattro sinko.

What do you call a boomerang that doesn't work?
A stick.

What is a ghosts favorite position in soccer?
Ghoul keeper.

What is a Cheerleader's favorite food?
Cheerios!

Why can't Cinderella play soccer?
Because she's always running away from the ball.

When is a baby good at basketball?
When it's dribbling!

Why did the basketball player go to jail?
Because he shot the ball.

Why do basketball players love donuts?
Because they dunk them!

What do you call a pig who plays basketball?
A ball hog!

Why did the golfer wear two pairs of pants?
In case he got a hole in one!

How is a baseball team similar to a pancake?
They both need a good batter!

What's a golfer's favorite letter?
Tee!

What animal is best at hitting a baseball?
A bat!

At what sport to waiters do really well?
Tennis, because they can serve so well.

How do baseball players stay cool?
They sit next to the fans.

Why did the football coach go to the bank?
He wanted his quarter back!

What is harder to catch the faster you run?
Your breath!

Why is tennis such a loud sport?
The players raise a racquet.

Why did the ballerina quit?
Because it was tu-tu hard!

What is an insects favorite sport?
Cricket!

What is the hardest part about skydiving?
The ground!

What did the spider do on the computer?
Made a website!

What did the computer do at lunchtime?

Had a byte!

What does a baby computer call his father?
Data!

Why did the computer keep sneezing?
It had a virus!

What is a computer virus?
A terminal illness!

Why was the computer cold?
It left it's Windows open!

What do you get when you cross a computer and a life guard?
A screensaver!

Where do all the cool mice live?
In their mousepads

Why don't aliens eat clowns.
Because they taste funny.

What do you call a fish with no eyes?
A fsh

How do you make a goldfish age?
Take out the "g"

What's the richest kind of air?
Billionaire.

What do skeletons say before a meal?
Bone appetite.

Why did the Skeleton go to the movies by himself?
He had no body to go with him.

What do you call a cow with a twitch?
Beef jerky.

Where do very smart hot dogs end up?
On honor rolls.

Why did the mother cat move her kittens?
She didn't want to litter.

What do you get when you cross a pig and a cactus?
A porky-pine.

What's at the bottom of the ocean and shakes?

A nervous wreck.

What did the mountain climber name his son?
Cliff.

Which runs faster, hot or cold?
Hot. Everyone can catch cold.

Why is it so hot in a stadium after a football game?
Because all the fans have left.

Why is a lost Dalmatian easily found?

Because he's always spotted.

Why was six afraid of seven?
Because seven eight nine!

What has ten letters and starts with gas?
An automobile.

Three guys, stranded on a desert island, find a magic lantern containing a genie. The genie grants them each one wish. The first guy wishes he was off the island and back home -- and poof!, he is back home. The second guy wishes the same thing -- and poof!, he is gone too. The third guy says, "I'm lonely. I wish my friends were back here."

What do you call an alligator in a vest?
An investigator!

When do kangaroos celebrate their birthdays?
On a leap year!!

What do you call a snail on a ship?
A snailer!

What do you get when you throw all the books in the world in the ocean?
A title wave

Where do cows go on a Saturday night?

To the moooovies

what day do potatos hate the most?

fry-day!

Why can't jungle animals take a test?

Too many cheetahs!

Peculiar Paper Tear

YOU SHOW A 4"x4" SQUARE OF TIS-
SUE PAPER. PROCEDE TO TEAR
IT INTO SMALL PIECES. NOW ROLL
UP THE TORN PIECES INTO A BALL,
SQUEEZING IT AS YOU DO SO.
WITH A SHOUT OF "PRESTO", UN-
ROLL THE BALL AND THE PIECE
OF PAPER IS WHOLE & RESTORED!
    BEFORE PRESENTING THIS
TRICK, ROLL A DUPLICATE 4"x4"
TISSUE INTO A BALL, AND HIDE IT
IN YOUR HAND. WHEN DOING THIS
STUNT, SIMPLY TRADE PLACES
WITH THE TORN PIECES AND THE
WHOLE PIECES, WHILE YOU ARE
GOING THRU THE SQUEEZING MOTION.

WHOLE
PIECE
HIDDEN,
DO NOT
SHOW

WHOLE PIECE

TEAR THIS

TORN
PIECES

TRADE
PIECES

What kind of room can you eat?

A mushroom!

Which side of a parrot has the most feathers?

The outside!

April showers bring mayflowers, then what do mayflowers bring?

Pilgrims!!!

What is orange and sounds like a parrot?

A carrot.

What did the man who lost his left side say?

Im all right now!

What is the difference between Bird Flu and Swine Flu?

For bird flu you need tweetment and for swine flu you need oinkment.

What is the longest word?

Smiles; because it has a mile in between.

What comes after a monkey?

It's tail.

What goes up when the rain comes down?

An Umbrella.

Why did the skeleton go to the barbeque?
Because he wanted some spare ribs.

What is the difference between a unicorn and a lettuce?
One is a funny beast, and the other is a bunny feast.

What did one magnet say to the other magnet?
I find you very attractive.

What's big, grey and goes round and round?
An elephant stuck in a revolving door.

What's worse than finding a worm in your apple?
Finding half a worm.

How do you stop a dog from smelling?
Block his nose.

What did the snail say when he got a ride on a turtle?
"Wheeeeeeeeeeeeeeeee!"

What do you call an annoying vampire?
A pain in the neck.

What do sea monsters eat?
Fish and ships.

Where did the spaghetti go to dance?
The meat ball!

What always falls but never gets hurt?
Rain!

How do you know that carrots are good for your eyes?
Ever seen a rabbit wearing glasses?

What has four legs but can't run?
A table!

What has no beginning, no end and nothing in the middle?
A doughnut!

What do you call a cow that just had a calf?
De-CALF-enated!

What are two things you can't have for lunch?
Breakfast and dinner!

Why did the computer need glasses?
To fix his web sight.

I run but I never walk. I have a mouth but never eat. I have a bed but never sleep. What am I?

A river

Why did the young cat get arrested ?

For his litter!

Why are rivers so rich?

Because they have 2 banks.

Why didn't the skeleton go to the school dance?

He had no body to go with.

What gets wet the more it dries?

A towel!

What is a TV's favorite thing to do at the the beach?

Channel surf.

Why were the police suspicious of the window blinds?

They were shady.

Why did the baker go to jail?

Because he got caught beating the eggs.

The person who makes it sells it, the person who buys it never uses it and the person who is using it never knows they're using it. What is it?

A coffin.

What did the math book say to the other math book?

I have problems!

What do you do when your fish sings flat?

Tuna fish!

What can you catch but not throw?

A cold.

Why did the pelican get kicked out of the restaurant?

Because he had a big bill.

Which wolf got lost in the woods?

The wherewolf.

What do you call a cow with no legs?

Ground beef!

What does a train say that a teacher says not to do?

A teacher says, "Spit out your gum," while a train says, "Choo choo!"

What color is a burp?
BURPle!

What's a monster's favourite game?
Swallow the Leader!

What do you get when you cross a hammock and a dog?
A rocker spaniel.

Why did the nose feel sad?
Because he always got picked on!

Why was Cinderella kicked off the football team?

She ran away from the ball!

What do you call a cat that ate a lemon?
A sourpuss.

How do trees get online?
They log on!

What is a cat's favorite color?
PURRple.

What did one chair say to the other?
"What are you sitting around for?"

I'm at the beginning of eternity and the end of time and space. I'm at the beginning of every end and the end of every place. What am I?
The letter E!

What has lots of teeth but can't chew a thing?
A comb!

What is so fragile that it breaks when you say it?
Silence!

Why did the banana got to the doctor?

Because he wasn't peeling very well.

Why did the orange stop rolling?
It ran out of juice!

What's it called when a snowman has a temper tantrum?
A meltdown!

Why was the broom late for school.
He over swept.

Which country is the slipperiest?
Greece!

Laugh Yourself Well

Christopher James

Branson, Missouri, USA

Chapter 1: Laughter is the Best Medicine

"A clown works like an aspirin, only twice as fast"

-Groucho Marx

Is the day coming when your doctor will tell you to watch two episodes of a sitcom and call him in the morning? Maybe not, but more and more, humor is being recognized as a powerful force for maintaining good mental and physical health. The idea that laughter is good for you is nothing new, but now science is proving it.

"I always heard laughter is the best medicine. I remember when my sister broke her arm. I laughed

and laughed. It's true, I felt so much better."

-Christopher James

Over the past two decades, the effects of humor on the physical, psychological and social levels have been taken very seriously. It appears that the humor experience has compelling and deeply rooted repercussions in human physiology. Medical researchers at a dozen or more medical centers have been probing the effects of laughter on the human body and have detailed a wide array of beneficial changes. Extensive experiments have been conducted; working with a significant number of human beings, showing that laughter contributes to good health. Scientific evidence is accumulating to support the biblical axiom that 'a merry hearth does good like a medicine.'

The ancient Greeks included a visit to the "home of Comedians" as part of their "therapies process" in their healing centers. Laughter is one of the four 'natural tranquillizers'. *Anatomy of an Illness* is an account by Norman Cousins of his experiences fighting a paralyzing and very painful illness, called ankylosing spondylitis, from which, specialists told him encouragingly, he had one chance in five hundred of recovery. Mr. Cousins is a remarkable man who wondered ... if negative emotions produce harmful chemical changes in the body, won't positive emotions like love, hope, faith, confidence and laughter produce chemical changes. This idea caused many doctors a lot of amusement.

Norman shows that there's now reason to believe that laughter counteracts panic and the effects of panic in seriously ill people, that it also works against the depression which itself inhibits the production of disease-fighting cells, and that laughter actually increases the number of immune cells in the body, including cells that fight some kinds of cancer. Cousins believed that endorphin's, the body's natural painkillers, are produced during laughter. Endorphin release would account for the pain relief and the feeling of being naturally 'high' that most people experience after a period of prolonged laughter. Studies show that there is a direct correlation between intensity of mirth and levels of catecholamine, hormones that cause the release of endorphins. There have been numerous examples that I have experienced where I have had high temperatures or been ill, and still have gone on to perform my comedy shows. While doing shows in Ohio I came down with a terrible case of pneumonia. I eventually found myself in the hospital and suffered through weeks of recovery. After being discharged I carried on with the tour, wondering if I was well enough to perform. What was interesting was that while I was performing there was no pain what so ever ... even then I knew my body was producing it's own natural pain killer, I just didn't know that they were called Endorphins

Through the use of humor and laughter you are giving yourself permission to self-heal. A quote of love is, "In life, what you resist persists." Humor can be a wonderful release for people, because if you deal with what's bothering you, in the very process of dealing with it, it will go away, and one of the best ways to deal with it is by using humor. Hearty laughter has a scientifically demonstrable exercise impact on several body systems; you could compare it to the effects of a physical exercise like aerobics. Mirthful laughter involves extensive skeletal muscle participation which Norman Cousins calls 'internal jogging'. When we have a good belly laugh our muscles are activated; heart race is increased; respiration is amplified with increase in oxygen exchange. Hearty laughter is followed by a state of compensatory physical relaxation, which lessens physical tension.

Having been involved with cancer patients, both children and adults, I have seen first hand how mirth can lift cancer-oppressed spirits, humor and depression are incompatible. With only the exception of the most severe degrees of depression, humor relieves the devitalizing grip of depression. It offsets, opposes, and diminishes depression. At times of tragedy, humans turn instinctively to comedy for it's depression-lifting effects. My grandmother's saying, "You can laugh or you can cry" is very apt to most people during depression. As a professional comedian I remember when the local economy was having hard times several years ago and yet I found myself with more work than before. Many industries and businesses had closed down in and around my home base of Youngstown, Ohio. I realized during those times that people used humor as a means of escape and to try and build their spirits up.

As a comedian, I have also taken my show to nursing homes with very gratifying results. Not only did I gain valuable experience that would serve me well in later years. Quite often I would get comments from the nurses that I made a person smile and brighten up who had not smiled since they were put in the home. The laughter wakes up some brain cells that may have been dormant for a long time, and that's healthy.

"Scientists say we only use 10% of our brain. Imagine if we could harness the other 60%!"

-Christopher James

So, laughter being the best medicine is more than

a cliché. It does change cells, it is medicine, meditation and marvelous. When people are feeling depressed I always suggest they go to a hospital or home and try and cheer someone up ... it's amazing how therapeutic this can be for both parties.

On my office wall I had a notice by Dr. Donald Ardell that read: "Wellness is too important to be presented grimly, living a wellness lifestyle is fun, romantic, hip, sexy and free, and people who choose to live this way are stronger, better looking, have higher morale, superior bowel movements and more antibodies to resist illness. Humor is the soul of wellness. In order to live a wellness lifestyle, you can't always take life seriously."

The research on heart attacks also raises important ideas about how we can use laughter. It is interesting that humor opposes directly those emotions, which have been recorded as being associated with precipitation of heart attacks. The two emotions they discovered were fear and rage. Humor acts to relieve fear and rage is impossible when laughter and fun are present.

One of the greatest things about humor is that it is creative. It pushes your brain, gets you thinking about elements of life in new ways, develops new insights, calls forth unexpected and ingenious associations, calls your attention to factors in an experience or situation which you hadn't previously noticed ... humor stirs up the cerebral neurons.

Dr. Kathleen M. Dillon, of Western New England College has added this to the research evidence on the salutary effects of laughter. She measured salivary immunoglobulin A (sIgA) concentrations in student volunteers before and after they viewed humorous and nonhumorous thirty-minute videotapes. Salivary immunoglobulin A is believed to have a protective capacity against some viruses. Dr. Dillon discovered that these protective concentrations increased significantly after the students viewed the humorous videotape. The concentrations remained unchanged after the nonhumorous tape. She also found that the individuals who said they turned to humor as a way of coping with difficult life situations also had the highest initial levels of the protective concentrations. Her conclusion was that a consistently cheerful approach to life boosted the body's disease-fighting forces. She replicated this finding in a study of nursing mothers.

According to the December 1989 issue of The American Journal of Medical Science, hearty laughter may be helpful in preventive and the healing process.

The article was written by Lee S. Berk, DHSc, MPH, Assistant Research Professor of Pathology and Laboratory Medicine at Loma Linda University School of Medicine and was co-authored by Stanley A. Tan, MD, PHD; William F. Fry, MD; Babara J. Napier; Jerry W. Lee, PhD; Richard W. Hubbard, PhD; John E. Lewis, PhD and William C. Eby, MD, PhD.

Dr. Berk says that this study "has shown objective, measurable, and significant neuroendocrine and stress hormones changes with mirthful laughter that suggest a physiological benefit. Laughter is a form of stress", Dr. Berk says. "We believe that laughter is a beneficial stress and that it conforms to the concept of something that Dr. Hans Selye called eustress - or good stress".

The carefully controlled study conducted by Dr. Berk and his colleagues has provided data that mirthful laughter can decrease or attenuate classical stress hormonal responses. Stress hormones usually increase during distress, or bad stress.

"Our data showed that serum cortisol, growth hormone and plasma dopac decreased with laughter, plasma epinephrine was lower in the experimental laughter group, and serum prolactin, beta-endorphin, adrenocorticotrophic hormonte (ACTH) and plasma norepinephrine did not significantly increase."

Dr. Berk notes that a "positive or happy outlook gives one more edge in the patient's behalf. Removing helplessness and replacing it with hopefulness do seem to have a place in healing. I don't think a positive attitude is going to be a panacea where you think yourself well. However, I think it can be part of the total preventive or therapeutic package."

In a more recent study which was conducted in 1996, Dr. Berk and Dr. Stanledy investigated the effects of eustress, related to mirthful laughter, on interferon-gamma (IFN), an immunoregulator. IFN is a lymphokine, a soluble product produced by some lymphocytoses that exert numerous biological functions including a variety of specific and nonspecific effects on other cells. IFN is produced by activated T cells and natural killer cells. It is active in fighting viruses and regulating cellular growth. Its capacity, however, to regulate or modulate immune properties is believed to be its most important quality. Gamma interferon serves to ensure cooperation between certain cells in the adaptive immune response. It interacts with other cytokines in either a synergistic or antagonistic manner.

They concluded that, "The precise role of IFN in human diseases and therapy is not clearly understood. However, we know that it is clearly involved in the defense against parasites, viruses (intracellular pathogens), and possibly tumor cells. It is interesting to note that new gene therapy approaches in cancer show promise in immunomodulation for the induction of antitumor effects. Chiron Viagene, an immunology technology company, has developed two retroviral vectors for gene therapy of cancer, one of which is IFN Retrovector. Direct injection of IFN Retrovector results in significant tumor regression in several syngeneic mouse tumor models. Additionally, treatment with IFN Retrovector enhances antitumor cellular lytic activity in mice, yielding complete tumor regression. This finding clearly demonstrates its potential effectiveness. A separate but related point is that a deficiency in the production of gamma interferon has also been related to persistent viral (EBV) infections. He concludes by saying, "Since many of these substances are capable of modifying immune components, these changes in neuroendocrine and stress hormones during behavior manipulation may turn out to play a significant role in immunomodulation - that is, changing the immune system for the better".

Dr. Berk then goes on to say, "As medical

scientists, we must express considerable caution relative to drawing conclusions. However, when combining the results of this research with our previous studies, an interesting pattern appears to emerge. As mentioned earlier, our initial investigations have shown that mirthful laughter is a positive stress or "eustress" phenomena. It is associated with activation of T cells, B cells and increases in immunoglobulins and natural killer cell activity. It is well known that IFN plays important roles in the growth and differentiation of cytotoxic T cells, activation of NK cells and functions as a B cell maturation factor (B cells are responsible for making immunoglobulins). Based upon this understanding, it is reasonable to propose that there indeed may be a correlative relationship (at a molecular level) between the presence of IFN and other components of the immune system. Further research, however, is necessary to elucidate these effects on the composite immune response."

What all this is telling us is that although stress is inevitable and necessary in life, the negative effects of stress do not have to be inevitable. Good Stress is a balance of arousal and relaxation that helps you concentrate, focus, and achieve what you want. Bad Stress is constant stress and constant arousal that may lead to high blood pressure, cardiovascular disease, and worse.

"I laughed so hard I fell off my seat"

No doubt you've heard this saying somewhere or it may have even happened to you. The above quote actually makes more sense that most people realize. When we have a good hearty laugh our entire muscular system relaxes, our body relaxes and goes limp. If you're sitting on a chair and you have a good belly laugh chances are that you may very well laugh yourself on to the floor.

Laughing For the Health of It

Think about spending a large percentage of your emotional day feeling negative. Think about spending most of your time around people who spend most of their lives being negative. It's not difficult to imagine a sinking, unhealthy response. Overexposure to negativity can make you feel sick. I believe it depletes your strength, making it more difficult for you to resist disease. Negative emotions might include anger, boredom, loneliness, depressed, shocked, hostile, defeated, frightened, guilty, sad, ignored, and hurt.

Now think about spending most of your day with

people who relish the delectable dozen of positive emotions. It gives you a lift just thinking about it. Exposure to an abundance of positivity can make you feel well. Positive emotions add a certain quality that enhances every aspect of life. Positive emotions might include joyous, calm, hope, cheerful, love, bountiful, kind, delighted, peaceful, happy, vivacious and affectionate.

"Laughter is a symbol for all of the positive emotions" Laughter enhances every aspect of life and is a symptom of health and well being. It is a way of getting off the downward spiral of negativity. Try the following exercise: Think back and remember people you have really liked. Name them and list their qualities. (Include relatives, friends, teachers, co-workers, and general acquaintences.

I'll bet you mentioned "sense of humor" as one of the qualities attributed to most of the people you like. Humor isn't for everyone. It's for people who want to enjoy life and feel fully alive. Many times after a performance, I'll have audience members visit me in the lobby. Occasionally, I will have a well meaning audience member say, "I usually can't stand comedy, but I loved your show." I'm often puzzled by this remark and try to imagine any person that simply doesn't like to laugh.

Laughter won't prevent us from dying in the long run, but it may increase life expectancy. It certainly adds to the quality of life. If positive emotions are healing, we should be getting as much as we can.

What things do you do that you consider to be healing activities?

Ask yourself this question: "What do I still want to do before I die?"

Well, what are you waiting for?

The Twelve Affirmation's
of Positive Humor

1 I am determined to use my humor for positive, playful, uplifting, healing and loving purposes.

2 I will take myself lightly while I take my work in life seriously.

3 I will not seek to be offended by other's attempts at humor. When in doubt, I will see others as meaning well.

4 I will express my humor physically, using my face and (when so moved) with my entire body.

5 I refuse to use my humor to camouflage hostility or prejudice.

6 I understand that the gift of laughter is a treasured gift, so I will laugh generously at other's attempts to be humorous.

7 All teasing and ethnic humor will be by mutual consent and will go both ways or I will not engage in such humor.

8 I will respect the forbidden subject topics of my listeners. I will avoid giving offence with my humor.

9 If I offend another by my use of humor, I will make amends.

10 I will be eternally vigilant for the jokes and absurdities of the universe, and I will share my observations with my companions in life.

11 In the midst of adversity, I will continue to use my humor to cope, to survive, to heal, to grow, and to pass on loving-kindness.

12 On the day of my death I will look back and know that I laughed lovingly, fully and well.

Chapter 2: The Psychology of Laughter

What makes us laugh? Theories on the physiological origin of laughing have been put forth for centuries, but there has been no inclusive definitive answer found. Sigmund Freud thought laughter originated with the smile of an infant falling asleep at the breast - the emotional expression of pleasurable satiety.

Grades of Laughter

The medicine of the soul, or the sound of its healing, is laughter. A wonderful experiment can be done by simply retreating to a safe environment and starting to laugh, and continuing to laugh, on and on for as long as one can stand it. The laughter, which begins forced, becomes genuine and torrents of secondary creations of various kinds shows up and dissipate. Laughter itself can also be a secondary creation; nervous or cynical or compulsively gleeful or destructive laughter form a range of social "offenses" between beings, or signals, which modulate the meaning of spoken language. Laughter can be assessed and measured against the heart's concerns and interests. Laughter comes in many forms that take the shape of a staircase.

The steps are:

1. Silent laughter, the laugh you have to yourself, a chuckle.

2. Smiles appear on the face together with crinkles and laughter lines.

3. The first sounds appear as chuckles and giggles ... the titter.

4. The volume grows and wry laughs, laughing along with someone.

5. Relief laughter

6. Belly laughs

7. Unrestrained hilarity.

Consider the sharp bark of the incredulous that

knows that nothing is possible; the scornful and hopeless snort which while seeming to be a laugh, is actually a blowhard.

There is the sluggish whisper of the grief-lover, who laughs only to show regret.

The grimy laughs of the sadistic, and the slimy snicker of the covertly destructive, are laughs that stand out as false as a cigarette advertisement.

The terror-stricken laugh: a desperate whinny. The angry soul laughs with a kind of despotic glee, the laugh one gives when he is about to erase the tribe of his enemies in a psychotic frenzy. The laugh of the earnest battler is more like a rebel yell, a brave whoop of triumph or challenge.

There is also a kind of resigned sigh of laughter that is offered by the bored, the whisper of Indifferent Else where-ness.

More in tune with the business of creating is the chuckle of interest, a genuine laugh of those comfortably engaged in what they are doing. This is often found in the vicinity of the Snort of Surprise and the Chortle of Delight, all of which are sincere, solid laughs with no deception in their bellies.

The Chortle of Delight often gives rise to the Happy Belly Laugh, a gale of wonderment and recognition, that thrives wherever Truth invades the Land of Resisted Shadows. These are all found wherever consciousness is nurtured by the presence of sunlight and strong interest in the future.

The being who has found many opportunities for laughter often acquires a taste for the Clear Breeze of Enthusiasm, a rolling, light, happy laughter that never quite dies away even when the owner is asleep.

Higher still on the endless ladder is the Quiet Soul Laughter of Sheer Action. Its quietude is the intensity of all laughter without resistance, thus needing no noise to permeate its surround. The Serene Smile of Flawless Intent is similar, only tranquil to the depths of all being.

Another interesting fact is that when we laugh the brain's pleasure centers are tickled which are connected to our perceptions. A swift shift or switch in our perceptions can cause us to feel pleasure, crack a smile and even laugh out loud. I had the chance to witness this first hand two weeks ago. Some friends and I went to see the Australian Body Language expert Alan Pease who gave a talk on humor and was discussing his latest book on jokes. At the end of the talk, I bought a copy of the book and showed it to my two friends. On page 24 their was a picture that when viewed one way looked like a person reaching out with their hand, yet when it was turned upside down it became something entirely different, in this case it became something very rude. The quick shift in those people's perceptions caused unrestrained hilarity. On that picture alone my friends both bought a copy of the book!

A 'perception' is the meaning or understanding that our mind gives to the information reaching it. For example, your eyes might see a small black object. It is your mind that decides whether it is a wallet, a checkbook or an iPod. In the Alan Pease example above, we had difficulty seeing both of the pictures at the same time; it would only work if we turned it upside down. As a comedian I relate this by not giving away punchlines too early. The best jokes trigger the switch at the very last word.

Do you remember the feeling when somebody tells you joke and then finally you are given the punchline, quite often there is that, "Oh, of course!"

Research shows us there is a physical reaction when a punchline is solved. Using brain scans, researchers have been able to watch the physical movement as great punchlines shift the brain activity from one hemisphere to the other. One moment we are thinking left-brain 'logic', and the next our right hemisphere 'creativity' is flooded with electrical activity.

Children and Humor

Why are adults so serious, why are we so uptight? I think I know the reasons. Have you ever watched children when they are laughing? They know how to give belly laughs, and they will often laugh at anything. They are able to look at the littlest things and see the humor in it. If I were asked to describe children I would use adjectives like, playful, fun loving, wild, creative and spontaneous. If I had to describe an adult I would use words like, professional, serious, reserved, business like. We see those as appropriate types of behaviors, so when we see adults enjoying themselves and having fun in the workplace we question it.

Children have a lot to teach us, if we are open to learning from and with them. Children can also enlighten us by inviting us to lighten up. Have you ever seen a small child whose out of character behavior immediately brightens your day? I remember sitting in a restaurant a few years ago watching a small child at a neighboring table. This tiny human, relaxing in a high chair, was perfectly mimicking those at the table. Every facial expression, every hand movement, was a perfect reflection of the accompanying adults that were paying no attention to the child. The actions were so out of context, I immediately started laughing and could not stop for the remainder of the meal. This simple scenario made for a great evening and immediately changed the mood.

According to Dr. David Cohen, a British psychologist, laughing begins at a very early age. Most babies start to chuckle by the time they're only 9 weeks old, some when they're as young as 29 days. At first, a surprise or bodily sensation triggers laughter in the infant. At 4 to 6 months of age, touch and sound usually produce giggles. By 10 months, the baby laughs at something visually provocative, such as a funny face. When infants are about a year old, they begin to initiate their own laughter by playing games such as hide-and-seek or pretend falling down. How often do young children laugh? Cohen goes on to say that by age 16 weeks, babies laugh about once an hour; and by the time children are 4 years old - when they absolutely love slapstick - laughter breaks out on the average of every four minutes.

There is an excellent book called The Optimistic Child by Martin E.P Seligman, PH.D. which is about a revolutionary approach to raising resilient children. While he doesn't mention the word humor, he does talk about "an atmosphere of warmth and ebullience, clear safety signals, unconditional love but conditional praise, and lots of good events which all add positivity to the life of a child". Obviously humor can be included in many of these things. He goes on to say that "it is amazing however, for a child to be surrounded with good things and yet still have a gloomy mental life. What really matters, in the end, is how much positivity there is inside his or her little head."

A study by Greg Garamoni and Robert Schwartz, two University of Pittsburgh Psychologists, did a study to count the number of good thoughts and bad thoughts that different people have and to look at the ratio. They counted thoughts in many different ways: memories, reverie, causal explanations, and so on. Using twenty-seven different studies, they found that depressed people had an equal ratio: one bad thought to one good thought. Nondepressed people had roughly twice as many good thoughts as bad thoughts. This idea is literally simple-minded, but it is a powerful one. "It is also supported by the results of therapy: depressed patients who improve move to the 2:1 ratio from their original 1:1 ratio. Those who do not get any better stay at 1:1." It is possible by using humor to help ourselves and our children have a 2:1 ratio of good thoughts to bad thoughts.

Believe it or not, there was a period of time when I worked as a substitute public school teacher. I would observe how it was a struggle for some children to survive in school and after school around the neighborhood due to teasing. They try to survive by being better than the other kids at whatever they were doing. Little children don't like to be teased because they're trying so hard to be perfect. And yet, all of a sudden as you get older, you discover that the people who can laugh at themselves and accept some teasing are really some of the nicest people and the most popular of all. It would be nice if you could teach a small child not to be bothered by teasing when s/he starts off in school, and to realize how totally harmless it really is if you just don't pay any attention to it. But, of course, it can destroy you if you take it too seriously. It can ruin your entire childhood. I'm sure we all have a phrase or a comment thrown out by a peer, friend, or teacher that has stuck with us over the years.

A tough sense of humor, a bitter wit or sense of cynicism, can get you through hard times. As long as you keep people laughing, you maintain a certain protective distance. And as long as you keep laughing, you don't have to cry.

Humor Therapy

Branko Bokun advocates the need for humor therapy in 'cancer, psychosomatic diseases, mental disorders, crime, interpersonal and sexual relationships.'

Bokun argues in his book 'Humor Therapy' (published by Vita Books) that the brain is also a gland, and that its glandular activity can be manipulated by thoughts or ideas created by the brains mental activity. The author blames the mentality of the adolescent male that pervades our society for resulting in high emotional arousal, 'inquietude, uncertainty and the fears of isolated and lonely individuals.'

Humor therapy helps us to realize that both unhappiness and gloom are infectious. 'That is why the pursuit of personal happiness only acquires a realistic meaning if it becomes the pursuit of other people's happiness.'

Bokun proposes humor courses, to help restore our inborn disposition towards playfulness, joy of living, curiosity, exploration and flexibility. His suggestions include:

-Develop a sense of self-ridicule, for instance by talking to oneself in the mirror.

-See amusing and happy films and plays, and read humorous books and magazines.

-Dedicate a corner of one's home to toys, as the mere sight and feel of them lessen tension.

-Hang pictures of children and animals on the walls rather than staid or gloomy ancestors.

-Find a hobby, but change it the moment it is taken over-seriously. Preferably choose a hobby that cannot go against nature's harmonies, such as sailing or gardening.

-Have a pet and talk to it.

-See life through a haze of analogies to memorized jokes and anecdotes.

-Repeat three times every morning 'I am not the center of the universe'.

-Remember the eleventh commandment 'thou shalt not take thyself too seriously'.

Chapter 3: Destress With Humor

Stress is an inescapable part of modern life. That's the bad news. The good news is that stress isn't altogether bad news. In metered doses, it can be helpful, it can even make you better at what you do, and help give you the competitive edge. It's the full on all-out stress that is bad for you, and quite literally it can kill you.

In his book Stress without Distress, H. Selye clarified that a person's interpretation of stress is not dependent solely on an external event, but also depends upon their perception of the event and the meaning they give it; — how you look at a situation determines if you will respond to it as threatening or challenging.

Because different people respond differently to the same environmental stimuli, some people seem to cope with stress better than others. Sociologist Suzanne Kobassa has defined three "hardiness factors" which can increase a person's resilience to stress and prevent burnout: — commitment, control, and challenge. If you have a strong commitment to yourself and your work, if you believe that you are in control of the choices in your life (internal locus of control), and if you see change as challenging rather than threatening; then you are more likely to cope successfully with stress. One theme that is becoming more prominent in the literature is the idea that a causative factor in burnout is a sense of powerlessness.

In this context, humor can be an empowerment tool. Humor gives us a different perspective on our problems and, with an attitude of detachment; we feel a sense of self-protection and control in our environment. As comedian Bill Cosby is fond of saying, "If you can laugh at it, you can survive it."

It is reasonable to assume that if locus of control measures strongly as internal, that a person will feel a greater sense of power and thus be more likely to avoid burnout.

What is Stress?

Stress is an adaptive response. It's the body's reaction to an event that is seen as emotionally disturbing, disquieting, or threatening. When we perceive such an event, we experience what one stress researcher called the "fight or flight" response. To prepare for fighting or fleeing, the body increases its heart rate and blood pressure; more blood is then sent to your heart and muscles, and your respiration rate increases. This response was probably beneficial to our cavemen ancestors who had to fight off wild animals. But today, stress itself has become the "wild animal." Untamed and allowed to run rampant in our lives, it can destroy our health.

The modern male's response to psychological stress differs little from the way our primitive forebears reacted to dangerous animals or other sources of potential physical harm (i.e., with surges of adrenaline, a rise in blood pressure and heart rate, and a 4x increase in blood flow to the muscles needed to fight or run away).

Our stress response is more likely triggered by overwhelming responsibilities at home or work, by loneliness, or by the fear of losing our jobs.

What happens when we are stressed?

When you're feeling overwhelmed — or encounter a major stressor of some kind in your environment — your adrenaline kicks in and your sympathetic nervous system takes over. Your body is suddenly prepared for action. But when there's no dinosaur to slay or damsel in distress to rescue, your body reacts with heart palpitations, sweating, increased stomach acidity, stomach spasm, skeletal muscle spasms - and increased blood pressure. This is OK up to a point, but if it goes on too long and your body doesn't have any "down time," you could be in for trouble. Researchers tell us that stress may play a role in the development of high blood pressure, though more studies are necessary to tighten up the connection. Stress also appears associated with heart disease, even if a direct causal relationship has yet to be proven.

Stress is not bad in and of itself. It may help to make us more alert, energize us, or give us a motivational kick in the pants. For years, actors, entertainers, public speakers, and athletes have known how to turn stress into "high energy" performances. Properly harnessed, stress can indeed work to our advantage at times. Personally, I can relate to this many times over. I have been in performance situations that are less than ideal. I arrive to a venue that is clearly not a good fit for my show, whether it is the lighting, organization of the seats, stage size, or other factors. In some cases, it seems like the wrong situation for my show. These situations often lead to some of my most memorable and dare I say, best, shows of my career.

Enjoy the comedy show...

Occasionally, introductions to the stage are less than ideal. The host, ceo, or emcee, has little or no experience with such matters. They are not accustomed to introducing a comedian or are suffering from stage fright. I'm often reminded of an introduction that beyond bad.

I was booked to perform for a large church. As they didn't have a stage, I was to perform in the actual church hall. After carefully setting up my show, I huddled behind the alter, waiting for my introduction. The audience filed in from their buffet dinner and the minister took the stage. All started well and then he announced that he had a serious announcement. Apparently, the church

secretary of 30 odd years had a relapse of a terminal disease and did not have much time left. He asked the audience to bow their heads as he led them in a very touching and heartfelt prayer. From behind the alter, I could hear sobs from the audience. Through tears, the minister then announced, "Our thoughts will be with the entire family, now my friends, enjoy the comedy show."

A somewhat less than ideal situation to be sure. I proceeded with the show, trying not to focus on the introduction. After the show, the church secretary stopped me and very emotionally thanked me for making it a special evening. What could have been a very morose and somber evening had been her chance to laugh and be with those that mattered the most in her life. I'll never forget that evening or how hard I worked to provide at least a little bit of healing.

Now, a whole field of research and study has blossomed to investigate the relationship between psychosocial events and the immune system. It's called psychoneuroimmunology. Its proponents think that stress is involved, in some way, in the suppression of the immune system, which protects us from disease.

If stress is associated with immunosuppression, then stress management techniques should be useful in preventing, or at least tempering, the impact of stress on health. Certainly, stressors in life may sap our resistance and put us at greater risk for disease.

Humor is like an inner massage providing a priceless ability to relax in the face of tragedy, irritation, and disappointment. A well-placed laugh brings us out of today's crisis to break the stress cycle and return to productive-solving. Humor can help us re-frame stress into opportunity, humor and depression are incompatible.

What causes stress?

Major causes of stress include illness, job changes, moving, separations and divorces, deaths in the family, and financial difficulties. But even joyous events, like marriage, the arrival of a baby, or entertaining guests, can be stressful. When I ask people what stresses them the most, they always relate their stress to work. People seem to put a lot of pressure on themselves at work. Humor in the workplace is not taking work seriously; it's about taking yourself lightly and your work seriously.

At work change can often cause resistance and stress. Not all resistance is bad; it needs to be honored, listened to, and dealt with. Normal resistance can be handled by interjecting humor to keep people laughing at their uncomfortableness. Instead of creating more defensiveness, humor allows a blending with "complainer", defusing the situation. Humor also provides a support that gives people confidence that things are going to be fine, that the changes can be managed, a feeling of faith in the future. Laughter reduces anxiety, and so it helps people cope with the stress of change.

Lack of communication can also build up

unwanted stress. We live in an entertainment age; if you do not find a way to keep your conversation interesting, people may tune you out. Effective communicators balance substance with style; they can be serious and humorous. Effective humor unlocks people's receptivity hence lessons stress; it also provides a memory hook for association to important information. If humor and laughter increased in organizations the amount of feedback a manager would get, the honesty and the capacity for people to say good things would rise. All the solutions to problems which lead to stress in organizations are within your own people, but the problem is half of them don't want to say anything, because they usually get knocked down. When you have self-esteem and things in perspective, you can laugh at yourself and your foibles.

"Managing for profit or bottom-line only is like playing tennis with your eye on the scoreboard and not on the ball".

Through my programs in humor advising, I do come across people who wonder, "what on earth I'm talking about, we need to get down to the bottom line, let's cut out the funny business". One concept we learn at school was the difference between process and product. Product is the end result, what you are trying to accomplish, while process is how you go about doing it and the interaction. People who keep on saying, "let's get back to business" are forgetting about the whole process.

How can humor be used to defuse anger?

An unexpected response can break the emotional tension and help move both people to problem solving. Humor can break down the anger cycle, but you will still need to listen and deal with the issue at hand. The safest focus of humor is yourself. Being able to laugh at oneself does not mean self-depreciation; it can be an acceptance of your own humanness. Laugh at what you do, not who you are, and the world will laugh with you. Only the self-confident can admit their mistakes; humor helps us let go of our errors and move on.

"The richest laugh is at no one's expense"
-Nancy Loving

The use of negative humor in the workplace can be harmful. If you've ever been the butt of a joke or when people say to you, "I was only joking, can't you take a joke?" then you will know that some people use humor as a negative weapon. Humor is a powerful tool.

How can you tell the difference between constructive and destructive humor, between humor that helps and humor that hurts, between "laughing with others" and "laughing at others"? In order to develop an effective sense of humor, we need to develop sensitivity to humor. This can be done by drawing a line between "laughing at others" and "laughing with others", risk interrupting toxic humor and finally by setting an example.

A list of humor that can be put downs include ethnic jokes, insults and toxic humor. These can create tensions between people and destroy teamwork; work against a persons self-esteem and reflect on the perpetrator's own self-concept and sense of security; reinforce stereotypes which are not true; minimize risk-taking, learning and creativity, invite retaliation and a focus on personalities and backfire, reflects anger, creates a cruel, abusive and offensive atmosphere.

From my experience as a comedian I have developed a style which doesn't rely on put-downs, racist or sexist humor. There have been tests, and I can confirm these from my experiences, that show people are likely to act in accordance with the model to which they have been exposed. Very rarely do I get people heckle me because I don't invite that type of humorous response from people.

While I do have fun with the situations my audience members are put into, I remain the butt of the joke. When people are "laughing at others" they are often being sarcastic, offending others, reinforcing stereotypes by making a single group the "butt" of the joke, destroying confidence and is usually based on contempt and insensitivity.

When people are "laughing with others" they are reducing tension by joking about human frustrations and faults which often leads to positive communication, encouraging people to relax and laugh, involves people in the fun and play, builds confidence and is based on caring and empathy, and creates a supportive atmosphere of fun and caring.

I would imagine that people who use negative humor in the workplace just aren't aware that it can be hurtful to others and eventually themselves. Their response is often, "Can't you take a joke?" They just aren't aware that this type of humor is hurtful. In my work I make people aware by being assertive, firm and taking risks. If you really want to kill a joke ask the person to explain it, this will definitely kill the joke and hopefully make the joke teller become aware that it wasn't funny.

Mental Health

Mental health is the ability to keep things in proportion. And what is a sense of humor but a sense of proportion.

Below is some advice to help with keeping things in perspective and ultimately helping relieve any stress.

1. Feeling Good About Yourself: Feeling low and useless as though you've hit rock bottom can be good because it means you're already at the bottom and is a chance to take stock of yourself. Invest some time in appreciating yourself first, because the more you appreciate yourself, the more your self will appreciate.

2. Less self-criticism: Self-criticism leads to a build up of self-doubt and worthlessness. Whatever it is you feel the urge to criticize yourself about, turn it into an appreciation of a positive trait. Give yourself credit for acknowledging a failure. Turn a negative into a positive. If you are being self-critical then don't look on it as a bad thing, be thankful you can acknowledge where you are.

3. Make friends with your inner-child: Most of us are

so busy with being adults we leave the inner child at home whenever we go anywhere.

4. Laugh at least Once a Day: Laughter opens up to let life's experiences flow throughout you. Open up to laughter and humor. You don't have to be a funny person or a comedian to appreciate the benefits of humor. There is humor all around us, take the step to enjoy it and go with it.

Ways To Cope With Stress

Bill your doctor for time spent in his waiting room.

Fill out your bank deposit slip using Roman Numerals.

Have fun putting random items in other people's shopping carts

Lie on your back eating celery; using your navel as a salt dipper.

Make up a language and ask people for directions in it.

Pay your electric bill in pennies.

Put your toddler's clothes on backwards and send him to preschool as if nothing is wrong.

When someone says, "have a nice day", tell him or her you have other plans.

Chapter 4: Humor at Work

A sense of humor is an attitude and attitudes are learned. We can change old ones and develop new ones. Psychologists say that people are motivated toward the fulfillment of basic needs. Meaningful work provides an avenue for satisfying many of our needs. Most people work because they have a need to pay their bills, they want to socialize with others, be recognized for a job well done, and function to their full potential.

The ideal workplace provides us with enough money to help us feel secure, enough challenge and recognition so we feel like we are valued, and the opportunity to interact positively with others. Part of this positive interaction at work requires that you take your job seriously and yourself lightly.

There are two types of applications of humor. There is internal humor, you with yourself, and external humor, you with others. Generally speaking, you need to develop your internal humor before you can move to humor with others. Like many things, we have more humor in us than we realize, but it needs to be actively developed. To gain from humor, it needs to be approached with a spirit of fun and the inner child in us all. A good way to start appreciating humor is to be an observer and a listener. This will help you to improve your abilities to size-up situations and actively put your humor ideas to work. It will also enable you to see how others use humor successfully.

10 reasons humor benefits you, your organization and your customers.

1. Humor is a good motivator. No one will enjoy all parts of a job, but looking at the funny side will keep the harder parts palatable. The least expensive benefit in any job must be humor. It can also be one of the most important, it should never be a crime to have fun on a job. During stressful times morale at work can take a beating. When morale is low productivity goes down. It has been said that a 15% increase in morale can result in a 40% increase in productivity.

2. Humor generates creativity - it greases the wheel for creativity.

3. Productivity can increase when humor abounds. Difficult jobs are made easier.

4. Humor builds rapport and can break down barriers

5. Innovation thrives when humor is present. Any time stress can be reduced, when the pressure can be released, innovation will thrive.

6. It makes your organization more approachable and helps build customer relations.

7. As a training or teaching tool, humor is one of the best. Using humor to network or promote products is ideal and innovative. I am currently working on a book showing people how to use humor to network and get more business.

8. People enjoy being around a person who is fun. One fun person can boost the spirits of a team of people, one fun person can give a place a boost of energy.

9. You can laugh or you can cry. Laughter is the best medicine.

10. Humor is a sign of health. Having a good

sense of humor, being able to laugh at yourself and at a difficult situation is indicative of a good attitude.

Humor is:

-Creative, healing, the youngest feeling, the oldest reaction.

-Very important to survival and growth as a healthy human being.

-Ability to see human-ness of all of us by poking fun at certain human traits.

-Humility. In the face of sadness, despair, poverty we can hope and laugh at ourselves, self-understanding. It teaches us we are not as smart as we think, but we are capable of becoming smarter.

-Provide us with hope, optimism, perspective, joy and energy.

-A major instrument in developing insight, establishing and maintaining positive therapeutic rapport.

-Humor offers an alternative to violence. Wit, satire, caricature and irony are available instead of bloodshed, murder and destructive violence. Humor teaches and reveals new understanding, humor at least gives us a choice.

-Humor is who we are. If your organization lacks humor, it is inhuman, it is taking something very special away from people. If humor is suppressed, other personal characteristics which are required to do business are also likely to be suppressed; in particular, mental health, job satisfaction and creativity.

Humor in the office

Laughter takes us back to a childlike (not childish) playfulness and spontaneity, which is inherently enjoyable. It is very freeing and gives us a sense of power when things around us seem out of control.

I am constantly amazed at some of the stories I hear from managers and employees regarding humor at the workplace. There are many stories where people are told that laughing with co-workers is inappropriate and that the use of humor with employees diminishes a manager's authority.

People who think along these lines are missing out on a powerful tool for improving people-handling skills. As discussed, when humor is used appropriately, it can help resolve conflicts, open communications, relieve office tensions and promote teamwork.

After years of working with executives, I am convinced there is a direct correlation between a sense of humor and effective administrators who use it to illustrate points, add color to meetings and spice up memos.

According to Mike Mescon, chairman of the department of management at Georgia State University, you can learn to become aware of the untapped resources in humor and to adapt them to your particular personality and management style. "If humor is just a facade", says Mescon, "it won't be effective."

Mescon's opinion is supported by a survey conducted by Richard J. Cronin for his executive search firm in Rosemont, Illinois. "Significantly, the corporate CEO's almost to a man, agreed that humor in business is healthy and important to the conduct of business; executives should develop a greater sense of humor in conducting business activities, and all other qualifications being equal, they would hire the job applicant with a better sense of humor ... I think the more secure you are, the more effectively you will use humor."

Psychiatrist Mel Udel agrees. "When I was an officer of Metropolitan Life Insurance Company, the most effective managers I knew always used humor. It's a good business strategy - in negotiating, for example - to disarm people. And it can also improve the work atmosphere in your office." Udel finds humor especially effective in defusing anger and lessening tension.

Many people associate intentional humor with giving speeches, where it can be quite effective.

It is a good idea to always be listening out for funny stories to build up a mental file of usable humor. In a speech the goal is not simply to be funny but to use relevant humor to drive a point home and to illustrate a problem, and most importantly to humanize the speaker.

I can never stress enough ... HUMOR IS GREAT FOR BUSINESS. Often the serious person doesn't take risks for fear of rejection or disapproval. In a business setting, this attitude can be counterproductive. I have this theory that if there was more fun in the workplace there would be less absenteeism.

Lack of employee loyalty can be a major problem in the business world - especially in the area of commission sales where turnover is traditionally very high. Humor can creep into everything from conversations, weekly sales letters to memos. Humor can be a tonic, and a constructive pressure valve allowing a person to criticize without hurting feelings.

Humor is not the only answer and will not cure everything, and does not fit everybody's style, although anyone can be humorous if the humor is adapted to one's personality. A person who is low-key needs understated humor. If you are not a funny person and feel uncomfortable making people laugh, you can work on developing a humorous personality - the ability to take one step back, put a situation in perspective, and see the funny side of it.

Workers who find the funny side of daily routines improve morale and increase cooperation. Humor can help turn around enemy relationships; we see a different side of them and they of us. Laughter is contagious and so is negativism. Which would you prefer?

My suggestion to people who want to develop their humor vision is to spend about 5 minutes each day standing back from things and just observing everything around you to get a perspective on what is happening. Look for the humor within you and around you. When you look for humor, humor finds you. If you were to imagine that you were filming a scene from Candid Camera and you have a camera in hand for 5 minutes, you will be amazed at how much humor you can capture around you. To develop your sense of humor call upon your other senses. Be farsighted and humor will introduce itself to you.

It is important that people take their jobs seriously, and themselves lightly. There is a difference between being a serious professional and being a solemn one. Hard work and humor go hand in hand.

How successful managers suggest view humor in the workplace:

1 It is essential to do a good job and still enjoy what you are doing.

2 My job involves interviewing people, humor plays a large part in relaxing the interviewee.

3 Laugh at yourself, so others can laugh at themselves with ease if something goes wrong. Because humor is so personal, and because people are so sensitive to the consequences of their attempts at humor, it's often safest to make fun of yourself. This makes it harder for someone to take offence. Self-deprecating humor is often interpreted by others as an expression of self-confidence.

4 Remember ... a full time job is only part-time in your life. Keep perspective with humor.

5 Encourage laughter on the job.

6 If you have a smile on your face, other people will smile.

7 Do not use humor at the expense of another or else it will backfire.

8 Looking at the environment, this tends to program us to push the laughter and joy deeper

inside until it's hard to find.

9 Humor is made from pain, not pain inflicted by laughter.

10 Know thy people. Shakespeare wrote: "A jest's prosperity lies in the ear/Of him that hears it, never in the tongue/Of him that makes it". What is funny to one person may be a social statement to another. Get to know the people you work with and help them to know you.

11 Use humor to diagnose. Because humor can be so revealing, I use it to diagnose the character of a person and of their organization. In my advising to companies, I always pay attention to the kind of humor I hear.

We need to look beyond job satisfaction to bring the best out in people, both in terms of their productivity and mental health. Looking at children we can see joy and seemingly endless creative energy and enthusiasm. As adults we probably feel those feelings of fun every now and then, but not as often as we'd like. We can look at our educational and work institutions to see why these feelings are discouraged, they are very rarely rewarded. On top of that, many people view the world as a very serious place, a place in which it's hard to find fun.

From my work with companies and individuals I have discovered the power of humor. When the feelings of fun can be brought into the workplace, they have the potential to make the organization stronger. Making organizations fun may actually be a good investment.

Is it OK to have fun at work?

Yes!! There are three elements which lead to having fun at work. Firstly are the people's intentions, then the organization's culture or environment and finally the management behaviors.

People who try to make work fun have more fun at work. This may seem obvious and very simple on the face, but this effort by people who do use humor at work is based on a complex set of personal beliefs.

People who believe that fun has positive effects in their lives are more likely to try to make their jobs fun. Other people feel that fun doesn't belong at work and so it doesn't have positive effects. These people are less likely to attempt to make work fun, and they're less likely to have fun at work.

Imagine if everyone at your work took as their personal mission statement "to practice joy on the path of service." If you can create an atmosphere of trust and support in your company, where people can honestly say that "the happiness of others is our own business", then you will have created a sense of team where personal jealousies and office politics have far less meaning.

The idea that "If I'm having fun I can't really be working comes from the old Listerine management model: "it has to taste bad to be effective". Work has to feel like work or it really isn't work. If it feels good it must be play, or something worse.

In reality, people who enjoy their work say they cannot tell the difference between their work and their play - it feels so much the same. To be passionate about something means to love it. Some people love their work, can't wait to get there, and they do more of it than people who dislike or feel indifferent toward their work.

Choose a job you love and you will never have to work a day in your life.

-Confucius

People who are passionate about their work are also passionate in the rest of their lives. They love to play. They know that meaningful work, a positive attitude, and a joyful perspective on life make us healthier, happier, more productive, and more fun to be with.

I have witnessed many times the power of humor in the workplace. Perhaps the best example was when I toured with a company, which hired my services to help promote a new series of products. I have worked for many companies travelling the country with similar projects, but never have I experienced such a rapport with a company and it's clients than I had with this one. The Sales and Marketing Manager has a great sense of humor and was able to use it to his advantage many times over. We travelled for about a month giving the presentation every night, and at the end of the night the clients were all saying how they have never been to such a fun presentation such as this one.

For what is normally something that can be boring, the use of humor was used to great advantage to help people concentrate and keep them focused. It was also used to make points, how can they forget when it was announced a new brochure was to be introduced I came out saying these are the hottest tapware brochures around and it burst into flames. The relationship between the managers and the employees was one of respect simply because the employees knew how fortunate they were that both managers had a sense of humor and weren't scared to show their staff they were human. Laughter and play and fun on the job can help create a culture of caring and connection in the workplace that is just as important than productivity and profitability. The organization that laughs together stays together.

The organization's environment and management behaviors are also important to employee's fun. Managers may try to create an atmosphere of fun but they themselves need to follow it through. When employees see the management having fun and pursuing these goals, employees find their work to be more fun.

From my observations fun is not the same thing as job satisfaction. Having fun in work and being satisfied with work are two different things. Although employees might be satisfied with their jobs, it isn't enough, the work might not be fun. Once you begin incorporating fun into your work, you discover that the deeper purpose for doing so is to help create a genuine sense of job satisfaction for yourself as well as others.

There are of course those jobs which can be harder than others to create fun. This doesn't mean that there can't be fun in them, quite often people haven't stepped back and taken a look at how to have fun. Again, both employee and management behaviors are important to building fun in seemingly "fun-less" jobs.

There are times when it is inappropriate to play around at work, these include:

Not Funny - humor that detracts from the business at hand. When a group is moving in a forward direction and everyone is getting down to business and on with the task, humor that sidetracks the group is inappropriate.

When Humor ignores appropriate criticism or feedback - sometimes you'll laugh off criticism or feedback and that is just an indication that you are not taking your job seriously. Telling jokes for jokes sake is not always a good use of humor. Being a professional comedian is different from humor in the workplace. If you are always saying, "I've got a joke", you are setting yourself up to be funny. People are thinking, "OK, I'm going to here a joke so it better be funny".

When humor is insensitive to the group - You need to consider who you are around. There are many instances where industry specific humor is right on target. Lawyers can joke about lawyers, funeral directors about funeral directors and so on.

Sarcastic Humor - if somebody comes to work and has just brought a new suit and you say, "Wow, that will be nice when it comes back in fashion." Sometimes the off the wall, flippant humor just doesn't work.

Let humor be sensitive to the group, let it be a way to build rapport, put people at ease. Let it be a way of expressing the truth in a non-threatening way. In a meeting for example, keep it brief and to the point, actually use humor to make a point. Use it to illustrate a point.

Earlier I looked at children and humor and discussed what happens between childhood and adulthood, why is our humor often suppressed. As children we are told to "be serious" and "don't be so silly". I think that sometimes we are afraid of what others will think of us at work if we act a little silly now and then or show a sense of humor. Maybe we won't be taken seriously; we won't be treated with respect.

There does need to be a balance to counteract the seriousness in our lives and at work and a good way to balance it is to use humor.

For many of us, our best friends are those who can reveal their true selves - including their silliest side and their sense of humor. I know that when people laugh at my humor or laugh at me being a goofball I feel great. Why? Because humor, especially silliness, reveal a very childlike and personal part of myself. In fact, the part that may be most fundamentally me, a part which has remained unchanged since my childhood. So when another person shows pleasure by laughing with me, the implicit message is, "I really like the real you." The natural high that I get from going up on stage and doing a show where everyone is laughing is just incredible, as I mentioned, this is my buzz and why I don't need to take drugs or drink. There is scientific evidence that shows also drugs can reduce a persons sense of humor.

Here are four types of funny people:

a) **Those who say funny things:** They tell jokes but are only as good as their material. Most of the skill is in the preparation of finding and remembering good stories.

b) **Those who say things funny:** These people get laughs from things not intrinsically funny. They use proper timing, dramatic voice inflections, and gestures to turn ordinary stories into hilarious monologues. They often rely on painful experiences shared playfully.

c) **Those who say funny things funny:** These people combine the first two, using good material told well.

d) **Those who think funny and who paint funny pictures in the minds of their listeners:** Their active imaginations are constantly tuned in and receptive to the humor others overlook. The world provides an inexhaustible supply of material for those who think funny.

Company Picnic Awards

This company had a picnic day which most employees went to. In the newsletter the following week appeared these awards which caused a great laugh at the office.

-Most Sunburnt Award

-Ugliest Sunglasses Award

-Most Enthusiastic Volleyball Player

-Split Trousers Award

-Best Volleyball Serve Award

-Late-Comer Because I got lost Award

-Best Tropical Outfit Award

-Best Family Uniform Award

How to incorporate humor and fun at work.

1. The first thing is to look at the people involved in your organization. Not everyone is the same in the way they like to get praise or acknowledgment. You need to ask who these people are, how do they have fun, what is funny to them? The more you know them the more effective you can be in using fun for reward, praise and acknowledgment.

2. It is important that management get in behind the idea of creating humor and fun at work. There is an old saying that says, the three best ways to lead are by example, example, and by example.

3. Your vocation should be a vacation. If you get great satisfaction out of your job then you are more likely to build up a good sense of team spirit. Feeling good about your work is very important. If you don't like your job and feel you are not getting personal satisfaction from it then you're in the wrong job. As managers take time to enjoy employee's achievements and personal goals, this will help in connecting everyone together as a team and is important in developing long-term emotional wellbeing.

4. Don't rush things. Change takes time. It will take careful planning but the work will pay off. This includes introducing ideas and also getting staff used to the idea that they can enjoy themselves at work and have fun. There will be the stigma that if fun is introduced then "professionalism" flies out the window. Start slowly giving people time to feel comfortable with the idea that the company is learning to enjoy itself and to openly appreciate its employees.

HOW TO USE HUMOR IN PRESENTATIONS

1. Do use humorous stories and jokes which relate directly to the topic of your speech.

2. Don't laugh at your own story or joke.

3. Don't offend. For example: a person without a limb may not think a one-armed paperhanger joke is funny.

4. Do make the joke clear and to the point.

5. Do relate the story or joke to the audience.

6. Do speak audibly.

7. Don't repeat a story or joke that flops.

8. Don't repeat a story or joke that works.

9. Do tell a story or joke about yourself.

10. Do use the name of living persons in a story or joke to which the audience can relate.

Chapter 5: Creativity and Humor

"Humor and creativity can feed each other"

-Steve Allen

I was always in the mind that creativity depended on the possession of a special talent which someone was born with, but I have recently changed my view on this and discovered that it is possible to switch into the 'creative mood'.

In the seventies, some research was done by MacKinnon at Berkley which showed that highly creative people were no different in intelligence from those who seemed less creative; but that they took longer to study problems and that they "played with them more" ... so the difference was that the highly creative knew how to switch themselves into a playful mood. In fact, MacKinnon describes this creative mood as being "more childlike." Humor is of course very close to childlike playfulness.

From my experiences as a humor advisor, I have discovered that comedy loosens up thinking and establishes an environment in which people can be creative. Humor stretches your thinking and you are forced to combine ideas that are usually not associated with one another. An example of this would be the person who combined a surfboard with a sail and wheels to get the sand surfing board. By combining things together and being creative they invented a new leisure activity.

The idea of humor is to take things lightly. If you are able to make fun of something, then you are likely to challenge the rules that give "something" it's legitimacy and even think of alternatives. By applying the same set of rules that make up humor such as asking "what if" questions, parodying the rules, breaking set, and apply it to problem solving, then you are likely to come up with fresh new approaches.

While humor may not solve every problem, it will sure put you in a more constructive frame of mind to do so.

The environment in the workplace is very important, if it's fun then it will be more productive. People who enjoy what they do will come up with more ideas. Countless psychology tests have found that many people think the best way to get along is to go along. Whenever people get together there is the danger of everyone of 'going along'. It has to do with people wanting the approval of the others rather than to come up with creative solutions to the problem at hand.

In his book, The Practice of Creativity by George M. Prince he says creativity is an unexpected astonishment, a vital triviality, a disciplined freedom, a familiar surprise, an intoxicating steadiness, a predictable initiation, a difficult delight and a demanding satisfier. George M. Prince used these compressed conflicts to describe "creativity", but they also describe humor. My conclusion is that humor and creativity are connected on a conceptual level.

From my personal experiences I believe that if you want to develop your sense of humor, one way is to nurture your creativity. Humor and creativity give us perspective, enlarge our boundaries, generate energy and help us lighten our lives.

In this time of rapid and unrelenting change, employees and employers are looking for ways to help themselves and their employees to cope more effectively. A sense of humor and joy in living can help us through times of change and crisis. We know that if we want to incorporate something new in our workplace we need to do it gradually, starting with small steps. If you ease into the idea of having fun at work and slowly help to spread it throughout your workplace, you will be surprised at how quickly people will pick up on the idea.

Healthy humor is vital to our well being and our ability to adapt to change.

Appropriate use of humor is a skill that can be learned. When we are learning any new skill, we start with small steps. First increase your own comfort level. Find out what things are funny for you and start to share that fun with others. Test the waters; see what kinds of things work for you and what things would be well received where you work. Take your cue from others when you are trying to be funny and see how it goes. If you sense that others are feeling uncomfortable, change your material or approach. It's OK to ask for feedback when you are using humor, to see if others are comfortable. Before long they will be joining the fun. Ideas on combining humor and creativity

Look at the world through the eyes of a three year old, a five year old or a baby. The sense of wonder that children have is at the heart of creativity. I discovered how powerful this could be when I started children's magic shows at the beginning of my career. When I became the magician I was able to see things through the eyes of a five year old, this ability shifted into my 'normal' life and I am able to laugh and enjoy life a whole lot more since. If you listen to children they ask a lot of funny questions, if you give yourself permission to ask such questions about things you will bring to life your creativity and humor.

Grab the bull by the horns and try out new ideas, be daring ... even if it's a step at a time. Find your comfort zone and then gradually and slowly push yourself half a step in the direction of risk. From here your creativity and humor ability will grow.

Creativity and humor often need to be warmed up before you can get straight into it; after they are warmed up they become energy generators. Use humor to start your engine of creativity and watch it flow.

I am often involved in creative meetings with various people in my business and always we end up laughing so much I have to leave the room, but out of this have come some very creative concepts. Rather than put down an idea as soon as it has been made, I try to think of at least three good things about the idea, this invites synergy and a contagion of laughter.

Be a kid again...

-Give yourself a gold star for everything you do today

-Grow a milk moustache

-Have a staring contest with your cat

-Make a face the next time somebody tells you "no"

-Ask "Why?" a lot

-Have someone read you a story

-Wear your favorite shirt with your favorite pants even if they don't match

-Do a cartwheel in public

-Hide your vegetables under your napkin at a restaurant

-Make a "slurpy" sound with your straw when you get to the bottom of a milkshake

-Stick your head out the car window and moo if you see a cow

-Walk barefoot in wet grass

-Make cool screeching noises every time your

car turns

-Count the colors in a rainbow

-Take a running jump over a big puddle

-Giggle a lot for no real reason

-Do that tap-someone-on-the-shoulder-while-you-stand-on-their-opposite-side-and-   they-turn-around-and-no-one's-there thing

---

Chapter 6: The Full Time Comedian

"Who is the more foolish: the fool, or the
fool who follows him?"
-Obi Wan Kenobi, Star Wars

With my career choice as a professional comedian has come new ways to look at how humor can benefit the workplace, and in many ways I see myself like the King's court jester, the Corporate Fool. I am a professional advisor, the confidant, and the observer. Outside the court, free of in-house politics and promotion and favor, the Fool is in the best place to see things as they really are and to offer alternative perspectives. If the King wants honest answers such as "How do things look, really?" it is the fool he turns to. The Fool asks awkward questions like "Why?" and "Why Not?"

The jester has evolved quite a bit since 1202. He's become a far more abstract figure. His court has come to stand for a place of mirth and frivolity, a place to temporarily set aside the trials of life. There are now just as many jester she's as he's. Teenagers all over the country wear the jester's motley hat, whether they can juggle and sing or not. Simply being a funny person is reason enough to assume the jester's mantle. Why so many more jesters than clowns? Could be just etymology, but most people would agree that the jester has a certain nobility in his buffoonery that a clown lacks.

The word jester conjures a lot of things to mind. These days, the image that tends to jump to mind first is an oddly noble, frivolous, jocular fellow. Due to the sweeping range of his history, the jester has become extremely abstract, and several different, unique "types" of jesters have arisen. Here's just a sampler of a few that I've noticed:

The "look, -I-own-a-jester's-hat" Jester: This not necessarily jocular fellow is best noted for his often out-of-place jester's hat. Often a teenager, he doesn't necessarily know how to juggle or sing, and may just wear the hat for the nonstandard fashion statement it makes, or because he thinks he's funny. Though not "fake" jesters, there are certainly more sincere jesters out there.

The poor-but-wise "Shakespearean" Jester: Notable for their nonstandard clothes (for a jester), these guys are usually historically authentic, or at least they try to be. They don't go in for really gaudy hats or clothes, and aren't necessarily frivolous either. They often sing and make subtle humor, so they're not really raucous, but they do have an admirable authenticity about them.

The stereotypical "I'm probably a copyright by now" Jester: This is the guy with the big goofy grin and hat with bells. He juggles and wears checkered tights, just like every good jester should. The "Stuffy" shirt corporation is probably trying to get the exclusive rights to him as we speak.

The "mystical-warlock-from-beyond" Jester: A purely modern creation, this jester came into being partly as a result of the jester's mysterious, noble aura, and partly as a result of the jesters image being used everywhere, often in fantasy and D&D-style pictures. Likely from another dimension, this jester wields fantastic and mysterious magical powers and doesn't do a lot of clowning.

The "Straight-out-of-Spawn-comics" Jester: A variation of the mystical jester, this guy is a total glamorization. He has James Bond refinement, a ridiculous number of points in his hat, and the ability to juggle obscene numbers of objects. Usually draw with dramatic perspective, he can do things most jesters only dream of.

The Professional Fool

I see myself as a modern day fool advisor. Don't be fooled by a professional fool. It takes intelligence, imagination, cleverness, and insight to play this role. The fool was consulted by Egyptian pharaohs and Babylonian Kings. His opinion was sought by Roman emperors and Greek tyrants. He advised Indian chiefs in the Pueblo, Zuni, and Hopi nations. He played an important role at the courts of the Chinese emperors. The fool was prominently employed by European royalty in the Middle Ages and Renaissance. Because of his ability to open up people's thinking, the fool has been held in as much esteem as the priest, the medicine man, and the shaman.

The fool had the license to parody any proposals under discussion and to shatter the prevailing mindset. The fool's candid jokes and offbeat observations put the issue in a fresh light and forced the king to re-examine his assumptions. By listening to the fool, the king improved his judgment, enhanced his creativity, and protected himself from going along with everyone else.

The fool lives and works by two key principles:

1. The Fool sees things as they really are

2. The Fool says things as they really are.

We can all be fools, we can balance our expertise and experience with honesty and innovation, if we follow these four principles:

1. Fools offer outside perspectives:

We often mix with people who are like us. We generally debate issues with those who already think like we do. A fool can offer an outside perspective that can generate new ideas and spark energy and creativity.

2. Fools see it like it is:

The Fool is able to see things as they are, no worse, no better ... just the way it is.

3. Fools are honest:

Out of seeing things as they are, comes honesty.

4. Fools are masters of communication:

Nobody will be grateful to you if you prove that they have to change - you have to persuade them to want to change - and that is a communication issue. This requires the skills

of listening, understanding and building rapport and the tools of passion and energy.

The benefit of the fool's antics and observations is that they stimulate your thinking. They jolt your mind in the same way that a splash of cold water wakes you up. You may not like the fool's ideas, some of them may seem too way out, too silly or useless. But s/he forces you to entertain an alternative way of looking at your situation. The fool's approach to life jars you into an awareness that there is a second right answer to what you're doing, and that you should look for better answers than the ones you've got.

"But the fool on the hill sees the sun going down and the eyes in his head see the world spinning round."

-The Beatles

Over 120 ways to have fun at work.

- Set up a bulletin board in your room that has on the cartoons, funny photographs, jokes or humorous quotes related to the topic at hand. Encourage employees to contribute work related funny items

- Court gesture: on a rotating basis, have different people assume the role of " court gesture" in your meetings. The adjuster could be responsible for providing and entered chives are or injecting some humor during a break. This might enable people to take themselves less seriously while continuing to take their jobs and responsibilities seriously.

- Create a "1st aid kit". A kit that contains surefire stimuli that tickle your funny bone, include comedy tapes, jokes, riddles, cartoons etc.

- Humor can be a sign of the times, of the times you want to gain name recognition or your company, of the times you want to make your company seem inviting to potential customers. Here are some examples that others have used. On the plumber's truck: a flush beats a full house. On a magicians van: warning, a magician driving, may turn into a garage.

- Make a conscious effort to look and listen for relevant and funny work related things around you. Write them down immediately. Eventually you will build up a file of suitable material for speeches and presentations, which is the easiest and most logical way to use humor.

- Occasionally sprinkle internal correspondences with humor. As Joe Goodman, director of the humor project puts it, "humor sells ideas and improves the recall of those ideas, why do you think so many advertisements use it?"

- Practice predicting stressful situations you might encounter and prepare alternative humorous responses you might use. By practicing these responses, you will more likely be able to use humor to defuse the heat of the moment.

- Experiment with jokes. Take one, adapted to yourself and your work situation, and try it out with several coworkers.

- Smile more. This sounds simple, but some people, habitually do not smile. People who smile or better liked. Take yourself lightly and your work seriously. After all, work is very important.

- Be aware of people's sensitivities. As effective as humor can be, it is inappropriate when it makes you seem insensitive to an employee's basic concerns. For instance, regarding salary levels.

- And perhaps most important of all, focus humor on yourself and work situation, not on other people.

- Learn to look for something humorous and every situation; finding the funny side will help you keep a healthy perspective. Think funny and adopt an attitude of playfulness. This is not a license to be outrageous, but an openness to allow your mind to make room for the uncensored, the silly, and the childlike. Take your job and responsibilities seriously, but yourself lightly.

- Be able to take a joke: laughing at yourself and work situations will make it easier for others to do the same in the face of their problems.

- Keep a picture out with your favorite cartoons and a humor journal of laughable experiences. Look at them when you need some endorphins to lighten your load. Keep a DVD of your favorite comedy programs. Set up an office bulletin board for workers to share cartoons, funny signs, anecdotes, and sayings.

- Look for real-life anecdotes that you can use to make points and talking with others. A good story is worth 1000 pictures and is usually more relevant than jokes that tend to be forced.

- Cultivate humorous statements you can use in talking to yourself in order to break the urgency stress cycle: this, too, shall pass "it could be worse I could be ..."

- Take time to life and smile on-the-job. Serious people are seen as distant, negative, arrogant, or intimidating. Rather than fly the slaughter, use honey.

- Acknowledge your own humor style and stretch yourself to develop and integrate other styles.

- Buy books with humorous stories, quotes, or jokes, and find some that you can personalize.

- Offer a prize for a week to the employee who comes in with the most appropriate humor for whatever is happening at work that week. For instance, the busy president of one company received a "take a number" dispenser as a gift.

- Put something humorous in your own office that also makes the point. One boss had a life-size picture of her infant grandson with his foot in his mouth, and she captioned it, "don't let our customers catch you this way."

- Another manager had a "crisis meter" for his door. The chart heading movable arrow with such readings as "all clear", "batten down the hatches", "watch your step", and "meltdown". He changed the arrow as a situation developed. On one occasion, two staffers embroiled in an argument were reduced to laughter when he stood up and change the meter reading.

- When appropriate, allow for humor in some of your memos and correspondences. Thomas Edison interspersed humorous sayings in the margins of his ponderous experiment notebooks to lighten the load for his overworked assistants. History hasn't diminished his accomplishments for doing so. Allen Piece in his humor seminar mentioned having a joke as a P. S. without the punch line. People will keep the letter for a long time and will more often than not call to find out the answer to the joke.

- If you hire a professional writer for your speeches, hire one who knows how to write humor tailored to your personality and style.

- Take a humor awareness course at your local college or university and their continued education program. You will be exposed to other business people and will have the advantage of contrasting the atmosphere in your workplace with other businesses.

- Bring in a humor consultant who can do some on the job problem solving with you, your managers, and your employees, and who will make suggestions tailored for your business.

- Take a humor break yourself, at least once a day.

- Committing to find, decide that you're going to make your organization a more enjoyable place for people to be. Your commitment to this will be among your most important contributions.

- Create challenging work, some top executives will tell you that challenge is one of the most fun parts of their work. A leadership expert recently confirmed this finding. He said, "Where there are leaders, work is stimulating, challenging, fascinating, and fun."

- Reward and recognize: being rewarded and recognized is often part of people's experience of fun in their work. Often, all you need to do is pat someone on the back and say, "thanks" or "I really appreciate your work and value you as an employee". Beyond this, there are other things you might try to create an even greater sense of enthusiasm and excitement.

- Give out "super person of the month awards" for the best contribution to the company's zero defects goal.

- Consider holding contests. Contest can be unrelated to the work being done, but you can also use a contest quite effectively as a motivating tool for creativity, productivity, and customer service.

- Employ fun people, recall that people's personal intentions are vital to having fun at work. It may be that those intentions are more easily selected and trained. So, try to hire people who are capable of having fun, who are interested in having fun, and who believe in fun.

- Increase awareness in the organization of the issue of fun, through training, and through your own behavior. This may sound obvious, but it's deceptively complex. Because we need to ask, "Why do some people try to make work fun, and other people don't?" The answer: personal beliefs about the effects and importance of fun in work.

- Witty words: include humor in some of your letters, memorandums, minutes, and reports. Inject it in your major publications: catalogs, brochures, sales flyers, policy manuals, etc. Include a humor section in your company newsletter.

- Decorate: try brightening up your office or meeting rooms with humorous posters, pictures, etc.

- Phony policies: issue hilarious policies or procedures on official company letterhead. Send out a crazy directive on sick leave, vacation travel or any topic which is applicable or pending in your organization.

- Pins and buttons: decorate yourself by wearing pins were buttons with funny messages. For a meeting which promises to be stress filled, wear a button which reads, "Save time... See it my way!"

- Staff development: offer a program on humor to all staff. Stress the positive benefits of laughter brings to an organization. Work with a professional humor advisor and/or staff from other "humorized" companies.

- Speeches and presentations: give boost to your material as well as your audience by humorizing your talks. Use funny quotes, amusing anecdotes, self-deprecating humor, and quirky observations.

- Unusual events: schedule "stress buster" events on days when the going gets really tough. Encourage all staff to dress up on Halloween and sponsor a costume contest. I have worked for a company who all get dressed up and open late on Halloween. During the deepest despair of winter, try a cabin fever break out day to lift spirits. Consider having a couple of crazy hat and tie Fridays throughout the year. Plan something crazy for April Fools' Day, national left-handers Day (yes, there is one). Celebrate March as national humor month. Be creative!

- Celebrations: surprise your staff by having their office colorfully decorated when they arrived for work on their birthday. Consider really doing it up on "decade" birthdays.

- Humor group. Establish a humor group whose purpose is to plan and implement a variety of different activities for dates and events throughout the year. Humor is infectious. Have as many people as possible infect your organization with mirth!

- Send jokes via the Internet or in the mail to your friends. With jokes you send via e-mail, mark the envelope "personal" or "urgent".

- Every month I sent one person a special certificate saying thank you for helping me or for just being a good friend.

- I give out "permissible to be childlike" certificates to people I meet.

- I wear fun ties and fun clothing. I had a special red and black suit made for those important business occasions.

- Make up fun surveys for employees asking crazy questions like "when was the last time you had the urge to wiggle your ears?"

- Listen to what children have to say and learn to appreciate their humor. They have so much to offer.

Make a list of the funny things you observe children doing or saying and let others read the list.

- If you have children, keep a humor log and give it to them when they are adults.

- There are examples of humor around us every day. Take notice of some of the funny signs in your area.

- Make up a collection of funny quotes and sayings. My collection consist of thousands of sayings, for example: "I feel good about this one"–Gen. George Armstrong Custer at Little Big Horn.

- My dentist uses humor to help me grin. His sign in his examination room says, "3 out of 5 dentists surveyed encourage daily flossing as a preventative measure for proper oral hygiene. The other two suggests that you "brush really, really hard".

- I love looking through old videos and photos with family and going back down memory lane. It always creates a lot of laughter.

- On the back of your door at work hang a notice or cartoon that you find funny, something like, "tell me again why I work here??" So that the 1st thing in the morning when you take your coat off you get a chance to smile and laugh.

- My grandfather and I often told jokes when doing chores. It sure lightened things up. Remember, "Time flies when you're having fun."

- If the office is feeling a little stressed, take a 1 min. "crazy" break and go into some song and dance. It will certainly clear the air and re-energize you.

- When frustrated with teenage-like employee demands, simply think yourself, "how could you take anyone who acts like this so seriously?"

- When I was a substitute teacher, I kept a notebook of some of the funny things students said, I would then share these with other teachers.

- Keep an eye out for unintentional humor in the newspaper advertisements.

- When I send out correspondences I always include an unfinished joke as a PS. This way the client , 9 out of 10 times, calls me to get the answer.

- I always have funny quotes in my wallet and checkbook, so I can laugh all the way to the bank. It also reminds me that I can laugh or I can cry when I see how little money is in there!

- At a staff meeting each week, have each member bring in a favorite cartoon of the week in a bag. When moving from one agenda to the next, pull out one of the cartoons, read it, and try to guess which person brought it.

- I belonged to a business organization who met every Thursday morning for breakfast. The first thing on the agenda was for everyone to get up and give a funny quote of the week. This always got memebers in the right mood for the meeting.

- Draw funny caricatures of yourself using other people's descriptions. Leave the caricatures for them to find–they will find you and you can share the laugh.

- I send postcards from my travels around the world to a friend who has a concrete gnome in his backyard. To this day he has no idea who is sending the gnome the postcards.

- Next time you are making lunch for someone, put a little joke or humorous note under the lunch.

- At times I am absent-minded. I make fun of this by asking very good friends, "Don't I know you from somewhere?".

- I collect stories of people who have played with stress successfully. I like the one from "laughing matters" magazine in which a waitress was being hassled by a customer who complained about everything. After serving him dinner, the customer quickly announced that his potato was bad. The waitress picked up the potato, slapped it a few times, saying "bad potato!" She then turned to the customer and told him to call her if the potato gave him anymore trouble. From that point on, he only gave her smiles.

- Put a sign on your office door, "why be normal?". People will always smile as they enter.

- Make up your own fortune cookies to share with others if you have guest over for dinner.

- I carry a picture of my kids and my wallet. It is a picture of 3 baby goats. I ask people if they would like to see my 3 kids.

- When I was in high school, I remember my teacher giving out lifesavers during test to lighten and sweeten what was for some a distasteful experience.

- Whenever I go away, I always like to look for toys, props, and humorous books to read and play with and bring back as presents for friends and family.

- A sign in the manager's office read, "You don't have to be crazy to work here...we will train you!"

- I have been to office parties where they still play "pin the tail on the donkey". It enables people to get in touch with their inner child and have fun.

- To develop my comic vision, I look for examples of humor and irony in the environment, then photographed them.

- Take photos of the office staff, place them on the bulletin board, input word bubbles with Post-it notes on the photos. Remember not to offend.

- Food can also be funding creates smiles. Quite often I'll give out lollipops, ice cream, and popcorn which bring out the child in us.

- Listen to comedy tapes while driving to work, you'll be amazed at how time flies when you're having fun.

- If you have to go to a meeting that is going to be on the dull side, tell them that you'll be there with bells on, when you turn up have little bells on your belt.

- Leave jokes and cartoons lying around for people to discover. A telephone booth is a great place.

- If you are at a tollbooth and pay to get over a bridge, pay for the person behind you and watch the reaction.

- Read 10–20 pages every day of a funny book.

- Include cartoons and funny stories with your newsletters.

- Bring in outside speakers for in-service programs on humor in the workplace.

- Leave funny messages on your voicemail such as "I don't want to bore you with metaphysics, but how do you know this is voicemail? Maybe it's a dream, or maybe it's an illusion, or maybe you don't really exist. One way to find out is to leave a message, and if it's reality, I will call you back".

- Learn to juggle, and then teach others at work.

- Learn a magic trick, and then teach others at work.

- Purchase a Rolodex and turn it into an instant humor resource. Write humorous or motivational sayings on each card and file them alphabetically by topic. Great to use while on hold on the phone.

- Recycle bubble wrap packing material. This is a great stress relief and an invitation for others to smile.

- Purchase a joke of the day and cartoon of the day calendar. Hand out the jokes and cartoons to people you come across.

- Send crazy gifts to friends.

- Put humorous pictures on your refrigerator door.

- Put your children's artwork on the refrigerator door. Encourage employees to hang them up at work.

- Incorporate humor in the e-mails you send. It will make the recipient take note of what you are trying to say.

- I love going out with my friends and talking about embarrassing moments. It's a way of sharing blasts from the past with blasts from the past.

- When driving with children in the car on a long journey, have them look out for funny signs.

- Create a list of good thoughts.

- Use reverse psychology for humor. I love the story of a person who was living in New York City during the garbage strike; they wrapped up their garbage like presence so that it would be stolen each night.

- Go and see live comedy shows.

- Record and video children at play. Presented to them later in life. It will be a legacy of laughter.

- Send incorrect birthday cards to friends and family, for example; send a 2-year-old card to your 69-year-old grandmother.

- Sponsor a staff development program on humor.

- Sponsor a costume contest at work with different themes.

- Make up a treasure hunt at work.

- Encourage a day where everyone wears T-shirts that are fun, with funny sayings, or cartoons.

- Visit the toy store at least once a month.

- Put up employee baby photos and have competitions were people have to match names to photos..

- Organize a paper airplane flying contest in the office.

- Write a laughter contract with yourself.

Abra-KID-abra Activity Book

Christopher James

Branson, Missouri, USA

Years ago, I toured doing my motivational kid's show for elementary schools. I called it the "Kids First" show. I met thousands of kids and to this day, still have some that contact me on a regular basis. Following, is my kids activity book that I gave out to the children I was lucky enough to meet.

Adding these pages to this book, have brought back so many memories of interesting shows, laughing children, and the wonderful people that made me what I am today. I learned so much about being a real performer during those years. I learned how to deal with any unforseen circumstances and less than ideal performance situations. Most of all, I learned how to perform for every walk of life and age. How to keep the administrators and teachers laughing as much as the children, and how to make them want to have you back again.

I hope you share these with a young person you know and enjoy the sense of wonder I witnessed from those stages so many years ago.

Abra-KID-abra

WELCOME!

Welcome to the wonderful world of magic, fun and excitement!

This is your **"Abra-KID-abra"** Magic, Coloring, And Activity Fun Book. In it you will find all sorts of exciting and fun tricks, activities and adventures to enjoy.

Magic is thousands of years old. Ancient secrets of some of the world's best magicians are told here. Enjoy having fun with your friends while showing them some of the amazing tricks you'll learn in the pages of this book. Remember part of the power and mystique of magic is in the **secrets**!

- The first rule of magic is **NEVER tell how the trick is done!**

- The second rule of magic is **never do the same trick twice for the same audience!**

- The third rule of magic, which really "should be" the very **first** rule of magic, is to **always practice your magic before you show it to anybody.** We have purposefully selected simple magic tricks that have high impact and are guaranteed to amaze your friends and family!

Please enjoy all there is to do and learn with your very own
"Abra-KID-abra!" Magic, Coloring and Activity Fun Book!

Magically,

Christopher
interactive comedy

Funny Stuff:

What do Porcupines say to each other when they shake hands?
"Ouch!"

How do you know that carrots are good for your eyesight?
Have you ever seen a rabbit wearing glasses?

What kind of cat shouldn't you play cards with?
A Cheetah!

How do you make an elephant float?
Add an elephant to 2 scoops of vanilla ice cream & some milk!

What has no beginning, no end, and nothing in the middle?
A doughnut!

369

MAGIC YOU CAN DO

COLOR SENSE

What the Audience Sees: You amazingly identify the color of a crayon handed to you behind your back only by touching it.

MARK THUMBNAIL WITH CRAYON

Super-Secret Tricky Method: Ask someone to take any crayon from a box and hand it to you behind your back. Make sure you don't see it! You then turn to face the audience but keep the crayon behind your back. Secretly dig your right thumb-nail into the crayon wax. Keep hold of the crayon behind your back as you bring your right hand up to your forehead as if concentrating. Take a quick peek at your thumbnail and you will see bits of crayon in it and will know the chosen color. Fake concentrating some more and then dramatically announce the color!

FROM NOT TO KNOT

Effect: A knot mysteriously appears in the corner of a handkerchief.

KNOT

Secret: Before your performance, secretly tie a knot in one corner of a handkerchief. Show the handkerchief but hold it with the knot hidden in your right hand. The left hand now lifts the bottom end of the handkerchief and places it in the right hand along with the top corner. Give the handkerchief a shake and drop the unknotted end. Repeat this three times. On the third attempt allow the knotted corner to drop, retaining your grip on the other corner. All you have done is change the corner you are holding but it appears that the knot has formed by magic.

THIRD TIME DROP KNOTTED END

JUMPING BAND

Put a rubber band around your first and second fingers so that it looks like figure 1 from the front. As you stretch the rubber band, secretly put all your fingertips inside the band. This is not seen by the audience.

Tell them the rubber band will amazingly jump across to the other two fingers. All you need to do is straighten out your fingers, and the band will move to the other fingers as in figure 3.

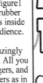

DO NOT EVER SHOW THIS SIDE OF YOUR HAND

ELbOW Grease

Show everyone a single coin. Tell all that by rubbing your elbow with it, you can change it into two coins! And you do it!

Before doing this trick hide a similar coin in your collar (fig.1) as you rub your elbow, grasp the hidden coin and, as you bring your hands together, you can show your audience two coins where there was once just one!!!

HIDDEN COIN

RUB COIN ON ELBOW

FIG. 1.

Acrobatic Clips!

Fold a dollar bill in an 'S' shape, and attach two paperclips as shown below. Tell everybody that the paperclips will be launched into the air, and in the middle of thier acrobatic flight, will come together and impossibly link... right in mid-air!

With a drumroll, pull the two ends of the bill sharply in opposite directions. The clips will come together and jump into the air all by themselves. Now you just need to catch the paperclips, show them linked together, and take your bow!

OPTICAL ILLUSIONS

Which One Is Larger?

Instructions For This Optical Illusion

1) Color both the shapes.

2) Use scissors to cut them out. (Careful! Get help from a grown-up)

3) Put one beside the other and see which looks bigger.

4) Switch places and they look like they change sizes!

COUNT THE BLACK DOTS

WHICH GRAY BOX IS DARKER?

A

B

(they are both the same!)

ARE THE LINES PARALLEL?

How Many Legs Does This Elephant Have?

RUBBER PENCIL

AMAZING MAGIC TRICKS

LAST STRAW

Effect: The magician's solid wand or pencil seems to turn to soft rubber. On command, it turns solid again.

Secret: Hold the wand horizontally in front of you between thumb and forefinger about a third of the way from the end. By moving your hand up and down in short quick moves, the wand will seem to become flexible and appear as if it were made of rubber (see illustration). This is an excellent optical illusion.

Presentation: Tap the wand on something to show that it is solid. Say the magic word and now demonstrate that it is wobbly and flexible. Another magic word and it turns solid again.

FIG 1.

Thread a length of string through a paper straw. Bend the straw- then cut the straw (fig.1). The string will remain unhurt! Follow the directions shown below and you can do this trick!

Secretly cut slit on one side of the straw, in the middle. When you bend the straw, the thread will fall through the slit away from the middle of the straw. When you cut the middle of the straw, the scissors will go above the string.

To finish, pull out the string unharmed, and crumple the straw in the other hand.

QUARTER BACK

Ask your kid brother if he'd like to earn a quarter. Tell him that if he can tear a piece of paper into 4 equal parts, you'll give him a quarter!

He will carefully do so... then demand his quarter! (now, this part is fun!) You hand him one of the 4 pieces of paper, and say, "Here is your quarter." (of the paper)

STRING

AMAZING **but oh so easy** MAGIC

PENCiL POWER

Effect: The magician makes some mysterious passes around a wand or pencil which uncannily starts to move on its own.

Secret: The magician secretly blows on the wand, which causes it to roll.

Props: Use a wand or pencil, and a smooth table-top.

Preparation: Practice blowing toward the wand gently and secretly.

Presentation: Lay the wand on the table and very slowly trace circles around the outside of the wand with a finger. Then, as you move the finger away, the wand seems to follow. You claim to have created a static field that pulls plastic like a magnet. The trick is that as you draw the finger away from you and from the wand, you blow gently on the wand. The audience is so busy watching the movement of the finger, they won't notice that you are blowing towards the wand, which causes it to roll easily on the flat surface.

VANiSHiNG RUBBER BANDS

FIG. 1.

FIG. 2.

Wrap a rubber band around the tips of both your middle fingers (fig.1). On the edge of a table, show these two fingers (fig.2).

Place both hands under the table edge (fig.3). Then show both index fingers and say, "The rubber bands have disappeared!" (fig.4)

Place both hands under the table again, then show both middle fingers. With a surprised look on your face, declare, "The rubber bands have reappeared!"

FIG. 3.

FIG. 4.

Tricks

HYPNO-PENCIL

Tell your friends that you can hypnotize an ordinary lead pencil and make it write any color they ask you to!

"Make it write red!" says one. So with a flourish, do just that!

Any other color is just as easy to do!

X-RAY VISION

Ask someone to thoroughly shuffle a deck of cards. The cards are handed to you and you put them into the box they came in. You now remove the cards, one by one, but name each card before removing them!

You have, beforehand cut out a little window in the box. This allows you to see the name of the card you are about to show!

RING THING

Tell your pals that you can do an impossible trick!

You say that you can push your whole hand through a finger ring you are holding in your hand!

Of course none of them will believe you! With a big smile, put your finger through the ring and poke your hand. You are 'pushing' your hand through the ring!

Appendix A: Photo Collection

Christopher James

Branson, Missouri, USA

Proud to say I have never fallen off the wagon.

Flashback to my rodeo days

Just say you are with the band ladies.

A 'magic' healing

By TYLER FRANCKE

TFRANCKE@BRANSONTRILAKESNEWS.COM

Several guests of the Showboat Branson Belle last week said that they were wowed by emcee Christopher James's magic act.

"He's really, really good," said Betty Cooney, of Des Moines, Iowa. "He's awesome. I still don't know how he did it."

But as impressive as James's illusionary talents may be, perhaps even more amazing is the story of how — and why — he learned to do it in the first place.

About 15 years ago, while studying at Youngstown State University in Ohio, James enlisted in the U.S. Navy, with the goal of becoming a nuclear engineer.

"I joined the Navy and sold everything that I had," James said. "I went for basic training, then I had an accident."

The devastating accident, which occurred while James was helping teach a children's martial arts class, paralyzed his entire left side. Adding to the injury, Navy officials met James after he awoke in the hospital to tell him he had been discharged from the service.

"I had to restart everything," James said. "I had to restart my whole life."

It was during physical therapy that James began teaching himself sleight of hand, determined to regain the use of his left arm.

"I was doing magic as a hobby before that, but that's when I really started doing it," James said. "Card manipulation and things like that. It was to learn to use my hand again."

After surgery, which installed steel plates in his left arm, and months of "frustrating" therapy, he began to regain feeling and function bit by bit.

"I hated doing physical therapy. It was awful," he said with a chuckle. "You're just sitting there, willing your thumb to move. I

'I leave that trick in just because I'm proud that I can actually do it. No one knows that 15 years ago I couldn't even move.'

Christopher James

Tyler Francke | Branson Tri-Lakes News

MAGICIAN AND COMEDIAN CHRISTOPHER JAMES performs in "Encore!" on the Showboat Branson Belle in March of this year.

needed something fun."

Although he still cannot use his left hand with the same dexterity as his right, he has recovered to the point that the injury is practically unnoticeable.

To this day, his performances on the Showboat include a segment in which he manipulates a card, making it seem to disappear. He said he has retained the trick because of the significance it has for him.

"I do it real quick on stage, just as a little throw-away," James said. "But I leave that trick in just because I'm proud that I can actually do it. No one knows that 15 years ago I couldn't even move. It's my proof that I overcame that."

While still living in Ohio,

James started a paper supply company, through which he was able to start performing magic at schools and birthday parties. Soon after, he started a school program called "The Amazing Kids Show," which at one point was being seen at 300 assemblies a year.

In the show, James would do tricks while teaching about values like patriotism, respect and overcoming life's difficulties. He got his first jobs performing at resorts, cruise ships and large corporate events from parents who saw "Amazing Kids."

"Everything goes back to that accident," James said. "It all goes back to me having this stupid accident and trying to do magic to feel better."

page 5A

A rtist keeps Jackson legacy alive.

Article detailing my accident that left my arm paralyzed and how magic was used as rehabilitation

381

Carnation Queen Maryam Jahdi, center, gets pushed back into a sumo ring Tuesday at College Plaza by her court. The sumo wrestling ring was set up at the shopping center for "Terrific Tuesday," along with other games and attractions.

My party rental business became one of the largest in Ohio and Pennsylvania and started as a college project÷

Salem business snaring big success with the Net

One of the first major retail businesses on the Internet, my company was recognized my news outlets across the country.

Business honors

Journal photo—Steve Schenck

The Salem Chamber of Commerce presented awards yesterday during the 1998 Small Business Awards Luncheon at the Timberlanes. Receiving awards were (front, from left) Vickey Honeywell and Diane Marsilio of American Standard, Exporter of the Year; Kathy Hendricks of Stamp Realty, Woman in Business; (back) Bruce Gordon of Gordon Brothers Water, Business Person of the Year; Dan Swindell of Valley Force, Business Adviser of the Year; Chris Greenamyer of Colonial Cleaning, Young Entrepreneur of the Year; and chamber president Will Stamp.

Receiving the award for Young Entrepreneur of the Year for turning a $500 college project into a nationally recognized company

For business, it's party time online

READY TO RUMBLE: Chris Greenamyer, owner of Colonial Paper & Party in Salem, demonstrates the giant boxing gloves that his store rents for parties. The entrepreneur started in 1993 with a cleaning company but has since added the party store and an online store, MyPartyPal.com.

My online business was an anomaly at the time. Very few retail businesses were using the Internet as it was only seen as a fad.

PRECIOUS SUPPLIES: Chris Greenamyer, owner of Colonial Paper and Party in Salem, displayed the few millennium-themed party supplies he had left Thursday. Several area party stores reported they were sold out of favors and paper products with the 2000 theme.

New Year's Eve for the year 2000 saw our company recognized as one of the largest party supply providers. Products were shipped to resorts, casinos, and businesses worldwide.

Magician will move from Stage Left to Mideast sultanate

By MATTHEW SCHOMER
Journal Staff Writer

LISBON — Fans of magic can prepare for a show fit for a king — or at least for a sultan.

Lisbon-based magician Christopher Greenamyer will present "Christopher's Comedy Magic" Nov. 12-13 in a benefit show for Stage Left Players.

He described the show as "a magic show for people who really don't like magic shows."

People attending the show shouldn't expect glitter, birds, lovely assistants, white rabbits and people being cut in half. Instead, Greenamyer said he mixes his magic with audience interaction and comedy: pop culture references, which have included jabs at Britney Spears, Elvis Presley and Paris Hilton.

"I tried to change the image of the magic show," he said. "Magic shows were always so serious with some guy in a tuxedo trying to prove he's smarter than you."

Greenamyer said he's been practicing the art of illusion since his childhood days. The former owner of Colonial Paper and Supply, he started doing magic shows full time five years ago, and now travels the country doing shows for colleges and businesses.

Recently, some Omanis have seen him performing on the

See MAGIC, Page 17A

MAGIC

Continued from Page 1A

campaign trail for President Bush.

As if working for the president weren't enough, Greenamyer will be traveling half way across the globe in January to perform for the sultan of Oman.

"I have no idea how they found me," he said.

Greenamyer

His show was the only magic performance picked for the festival in Oman, which he said goes on for about a month-and-a-half.

While he has received awards from the Magicians Alliance of Eastern States — for Best Comedy Act, Best Stage Act and Most Original Act — he said the festival will be his first time performing for royalty.

"Royalty's not very common," he said.

Although performing for a sultan seems like a much higher honor than performing for a college audience, business group or benefit show, Greenamyer every performance the same.

"Tonight I'm working at church banquet," he said Friday. "They'll get the same show as everyone else."

He said there's no reason for him to change the show for a particular audience because all sorts of people enjoy seeing it.

"Everyone has the same reaction to the show," he said. "They're all like little kids when they see the show."

Greenamyer's performance will be shown at 7 p.m. Nov. 12-13 at the Outreach Center, Lisbon. All tickets are $8.

I was honored to be asked to perform for the sultan of Oman as one of only two American performers.

Magician involves audience in his different kind of act

By THOMAS HARPER
The Review

Magician Chris Greenamyer, standing, teaches Katelyn Corns of Louisville how to do a magic trick. Greenamyer is at Texas Roadhouse in Alliance every Monday evening involving his audience in his act.

Funny faces

Man turns malady into magic act

The Audience Won't Just See The Show They Will Be The Show

My Branson career started in 2006

My cast of characters developed for America's Got Talent.

**Working on my America's Got Talent Arial Card Manipulation act.
Due to an accident, I had to bow out at the very last minute.**

Performing in South Korea for a state television show in 2009.

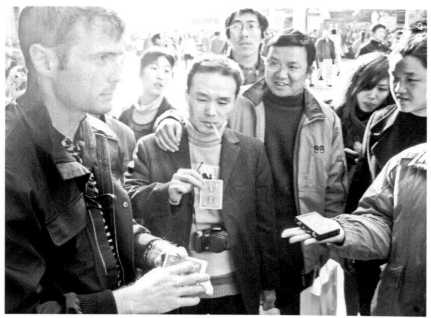

A photo from my CCTV appearance that was seen by 1.2 billion viewers in Asia.

A day on the beach in Cambodia performing a free impromptu show for the locals, easily ranks as one of the best days of my life.

My oldest daughter showing her creative baby sitting method for the twin, thanks to a little Photoshop.

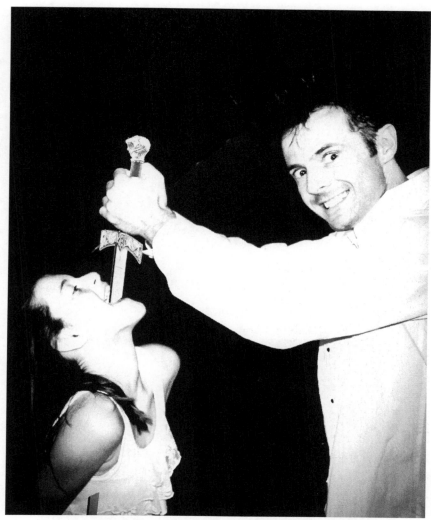

taking my daughter out to dinner thanks to Photoshop.

Magical swimming lessons with dad

Just for fun, we decided to swap faces.

2003 vs. 2012

Always an important part of the show, here are photos of my
daughter and I about 10 years apart.

Twins born January 16, 2012, about two and half months early.

2012

2013

2014

This is how Cassandra would react to her name when she was a baby. It never fails to make me laugh.

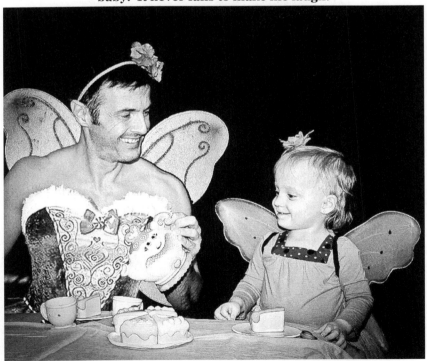

2014 tea party with Cassandra. There is always time for tea.

Saving the world with Alexander Logan, My favorite superhero.

CONTACT INFORMATION:

I want your help, please let me know your favorite jokes by emailing me at the website below.

Christopher has a huge online collection of videos on YouTube. Please be sure to visit the website and subscribe.

Share your own personal stories and jokes with Christopher.

funnyhypermagic.com

Be sure to visit the Facebook fan page, follow on Twitter, and Instagram and anything else that comes out in the future.

13580761R00227

Made in the USA
San Bernardino, CA
29 July 2014